Pagan Portals
Runes

Pagan Portals
Runes

Kylie Holmes

Winchester, UK
Washington, USA

First published by Moon Books, 2013
Moon Books is an imprint of John Hunt Publishing Ltd., Laurel House, Station Approach,
Alresford, Hants, SO24 9JH, UK
office1@jhpbooks.net
www.johnhuntpublishing.com
www.moon-books.net

For distributor details and how to order please visit the 'Ordering' section on our website.

Text copyright: Kylie Holmes 2013

ISBN: 978 1 84694 531 1

A CIP catalogue record for this book is available from the British Library.

Design: Stuart Davies
Illustrations: Nicola Stonehouse

Printed and bound by CPI Group (UK) Ltd, Croydon, CR0 4YY

We operate a distinctive and ethical publishing philosophy in all
areas of our business, from our global network of authors to
production and worldwide distribution.

CONTENTS

Acknowledgements

I am especially grateful to Ruth White for the continued inspiration and encouragement to keep writing this book. Thank you for encouraging my spiritual growth and finding my inner power. To Gildas, thank you for the continuation of our work and contact. Thank you both for your love, blessing, healing and support at all times.

Blessed Be x

Thank you Jade and Amba for your contribution in drawing the Rune symbols. Lots of love to you both Mum. Blessed Be x

Thank you Nicola for your contribution in the illustrations of the Rune Symbols.

Introduction

At a glance, the Rune Stones seem to be daunting, difficult to understand and you may feel overloaded with too much information. I feel that the best way to learn this ancient art form is to remember that *'there are no rules'*, and *'there is no wrong way or right way to learn the Runes'*. From my own experience, the Rune Stone meanings are only there for you to tap into your own intuition; you can let the Runes teach you what they are about.

If you've just begun your spiritual journey, you can boost the process whilst casting one Rune a day. First thing in the morning, leave the chosen Rune out, open up your blank journal and jot down whatever inspirational words come to you during the day. That's how I learned the Runes, and I was amazed almost daily by the insights these simple tiles provide. By then, I had been using Astrology and Tarot for years, and found it hard to believe that such a *'simple'* tool could be so profound.

I now always use the Tarot, Angel cards, various different Divination cards and the Rune Stones on my spiritual journey, especially when I ask myself, *'What are the lessons I need to learn from certain situations?'*

For me, every spiritual journey begins with the awakening, the desire to know what lies beyond material possessions. Life for me is like a journey within a journey, like chapters of a book; and at the end of each chapter, the book still remains to be completed. Each new chapter marks a beginning and an end: the end of one pattern, but also the beginning of a new higher understanding. With every positive lesson, however, as we know well, comes some form of negativity. So as you graduate from one level to another, you will often find yourself in a fury of emotions, good and bad. We have to remember that these are the lessons and until we learn to take control and break out of recurring patterns, the pattern will continue to occur, each time with greater intensity, until we consciously break out of it.

I would like to point out that the book I have written does not teach you the reverse meanings of each Rune. From the beginning, I made it a personal rule to myself never to do reversals, as I felt that learning the meanings of twenty-four Runes on their own was hard enough, without learning another twenty-four meanings. The reason for this is because I feel that not all readers do reversals. And if you're a beginner, it's probably a good idea to avoid them until you're pretty confident in your readings. Reversals take time and practice.

I also know from experience that when I am casting the Runes for clients they often get nervous when they see them reversed. In old-fashioned books on Runes, a reversed Rune meant doom and gloom and so, not surprisingly, nothing can turn a casting into a downer like a spread with a lot of reversed Runes. I have not included reversed Rune meanings in the meanings of the Runes because I personally do not use them. If you'd like more information on the reversed meanings of the Runes, then you may have to find a book that contains that information.

We all perceive things differently to the people around us, and it is the same way for the Rune interpretations written in this book. We each see something unique in each individual Rune. Focus on what you **FEEL** is the right interpretation for **YOU** and **TRUST** your intuition.

Practise, practise, practise and remember – the best teacher is **YOU**.

Blessed Be

Kylie

Chapter One

Origin of the Runes

Magic is believing in yourself; if you can do that,
you can make anything happen.
Johann Wolfgang von Goethe

In the Beginning

Since ancient times, our ancestors have used symbols to communicate with the outside world. They learned from observing all aspects of nature and adapted to changes in their lives in order to survive. They also used many different symbols and signs for divination and magic.

It is not known how old Runes are, but Rune markings appear on cave paintings dated from about 1330 BC. Runes fell into disuse as Roman alphabets became the preferred script of most of Europe.

Runic lettering first appeared among German tribes in Central and Eastern Europe. The Anglo-Saxon Runes are descended from the Elder Futhark, which originated in Scandinavia. They were also used by the northern Germanic tribes of Sweden, Norway, Denmark and Northern Germany.

Runes were used long before the concept of writing was around. Our ancestors saw Runes as powerful aids to divination and magic, able to influence the forces of nature and work charms of fertility and healing. Runes were also used in casting spells, to gain a kiss from a would-be loved one or to pay back an enemy.

Runes are actually alphabetic symbols used for writing. They were found on door posts, property markers, swords, shields, tombstones and even on Viking warships. The Norse used Runic characters mostly for practical purposes, such as marking graves, identifying property, combs or helmets, making calendars and encoding secret messages.

The Elder Futhark – ca. 150 to 800 AD

The Elder Futhark is sometimes known as *'Common Germanic Futhark'* or Longer Rune-Row.

The Elder Futhark is the oldest version of Runic lettering. It first emerged around 200 AD and was used in the parts of Europe which were home to the Germanic people, including Scandinavia. It was known as the Futhark after the first six Runes – Fehu, Uruz, THurisaz, Ansuz, Raido, and Kauno.

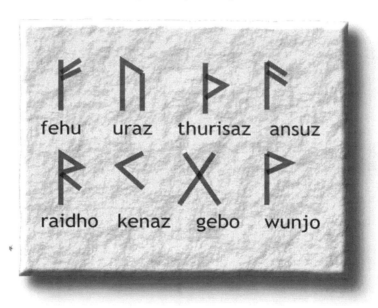

It is known that the Germanic peoples in Europe used pictographic symbols that were scratched into rocks. As the Runes consisted of straight lines, it made them easier to carve into wood or stone.

By 400 AD, use of a common set of twenty-four Runes (beginning with F and ending with O) had spread across Northern Europe.

As time passed, new Runes were added as the need arose; at different times and locations, various versions of the Futhark emerged, including up to thirty-eight symbols. Gradually, the twenty-four Anglo-Saxon Futhark became standard and was grouped into three sets of eight, known as Aetts.

The Younger Futhark – 800 to 1110 AD

The Younger Futhark is also known as the *'Scandinavian Runes'* and is believed to have been in use from around about 800 AD. It was the main alphabet in Norway, Sweden and Denmark throughout the Viking Age.

The forms of the Runes were altered and made easier to understand at a time when there were phonetic changes to the spoken language. Nine of the original Elder Futhark were also dropped.

The Younger Futhark is a reduced form of the Elder Futhark comprising of only 16 characters and divided into two sets, Long Branch (Danish) and Short Twig (Swedish/Norwegian) Runes.

The difference between the two versions has been the subject of controversy. It is believed that the Long Branch Runes were used for stone carvings and the Short Branch Runes were in everyday use for private and officially carved messages on wood.

Long Branch (top line)

(also called Danish Runes, even though Swedes and Norwegians used it)

Short Twig or Rök Runes (middle line)

(also called Swedish-Norwegian Runes, even though the Danish used it)

The bottom line in the diagram below shows the Runes sounds.

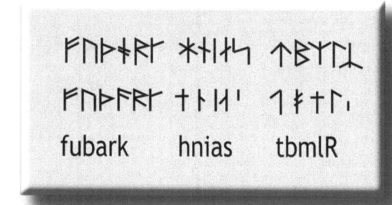

The Younger Futhark became known in Europe as the 'Alphabet of the Norsemen' and was studied and used for trade and diplomatic contacts.

Anglo-Saxon Futhorc – 400 to 1100 AD

The Anglo-Saxon Futhorc descended from the Elder Futhark and contained between 26 and 33 Runes.

Runes were brought to Britain in the 5th century by the Angles, Saxons, Jutes and Frisians. Extra letters were added to the Runic lettering to write Anglo-Saxon/Old English and the Anglo-Saxon Futhorc was developed.

Runic inscriptions are mostly found on jewellery, weapons, stones and other objects. Very few examples of Runic writing on manuscripts have survived.

In the beginning, the Futhorc thrived as a writing system.

However, its developing complexity led to increasingly complicated forms that must have been more difficult to carve and it did
not survive. The Latin alphabet replaced the Futhorc around the
9th century, and did not survive much past the Norman Conquest
of 1066. The Futhorc continued to be used in Scandinavia until
1600.

Creation of the Runes

There have been many theories initiated over who created the
Runes. One I have come across many times is about the God
Odin.

In Norse mythology, Odin (also known as Woden or Wotan) is
the chief God. Odin and his wife, Frigg, are rulers of Asgard,
which is one of the Nine Worlds. Odin is a son of Bor and Bestla.
Odin is a God of war and death, but also the God of poetry and
wisdom. Odin had many sons, the most memorable one being
Thor, God of thunder.

Odin's quest for knowledge was never ending. Norse legends
and myths tell tales of him wandering the world in search of
knowledge on his eight-legged white horse, Sleipnir. He also had
two ravens, Hugin (thought) and Munin (memory), who sat on
his shoulders and circled the Earth each day, seeing all and then
flying home at night to report what they had learnt.

On his travels, Odin met three women called Norns sitting at
a well, busy spinning threads of fate for the Gods and mankind.
As they spun their yarns, Urd, Verdandi and Skuld revealed to
Odin many secrets of the distant past and the future. Odin was
keen to learn more about seeing into the future, and the three
sisters pointed him to the Giant Mimir at the Spring of Wisdom.
Mimir is the giant in Norse mythology who guards the 'Well of the
Highest Wisdom', situated in Jotunheim under the roots of
Yggdrasil: the World Tree.

Odin rode to Jotunheim to meet the Giant Mimir, but Mimir
did not want to give his knowledge so easily, so Odin pledged his

left eye to Mimir for the privilege of drinking from the spring so that he could be shown the mysteries of this world.

Odin was not fully satisfied in his quest for wisdom and left. He travelled through the desolate heaths and eventually got caught in the branches of an ash tree. As he tried to free himself, he was wounded by his spear (called *'Gugnir'*) and Odin hung between heaven and earth. His horse, Sleipnir, came to help and his ravens, *'Hugin'* and *'Munin'*, flew around him and brought the world's thoughts to him.

For nine days and nine nights, he hung impaled on the World Tree, Yggdrasil, without food or drink. In a flash of insight, he saw that there was writing on the rocks below him and derived wisdom from this writing. He bent down deeply from the tree, took up his sword and cut the symbols into the trunk. He fell down from the tree and called Sleipnir to take him to Valhalla, the castle of the Gods. Odin then passed on this learned knowledge to mankind.

The Word Rune

The word *'Rune'* derives from the Old Norse and Old English, *'run'*, which means *'mystery'* or *'secret'*. These two meanings also appear in Old English *'rūn'*, the ancestor of our word. The direct descendants of Old English *'rūn'* are the archaic verb, *'round'* (whisper, talk in secret) and the obsolete noun, *'roun'* (whispering, secret talk).

Johannes Thomae Bureus Agrivillensis

Johannes Thomae Bureus Agrivillensis or Johan Bure, as he was known (1568 - 1652), was born in Åkerby near the city of Uppsala in Sweden. He was a son of a Lutheran parish priest. He had a good education in Uppsala and Stockholm and later studied in Germany and Italy. In 1595, he studied theology; in 1602 he became a professor; and from 1603 on, royal antiquarian. Bureus died a cripple in 1652.

During his studies, Bureus learned Latin and Hebrew. In 1591, he got a medieval magic book from his father-in-law, Mårten Bång, and got interested in Cabbala.

In 1593, Bureus became a civil servant and was appointed editor of religious texts in Stockholm. Just before he moved there, Bureus ran into a Rune stone that aroused his curiosity. He lived in an area that had many Rune stones, but he never really noticed them before he saw the stone in front of the Cistercian cloister of Riddarholm. He was captivated by the strange scripts and wanted to learn how to read them. He travelled the province of Dalarne and learned to read the Runes from the local farmers. In 1599 and 1600, Bureus made an extensive trip through his native country to find more Rune stones so he could write down, translate and interpret the texts. Bureus viewed Runes as holy and magical in a cabbalistic sense.

During his life, he was a Runic scholar who was interested in Rosicrucianism, which is the theology of a secret society of mystics. It is said to have been founded in late medieval Germany by Christian Rosenkreuz. He was also royal librarian, tutor and advisor of King Gustavus Adolphus of Sweden, who also assigned him to translate certain stones.

He combined his runic and esoteric interests with his own Runic system, which he called the '*Adalruna*', and in 1611, he published his first book in the Swedish language, *Svenska ABC boken medh runor*, using the Runic lettering and Latin script.

Olof Rudbeck Sr

Olof Rudbeck Sr (1630 - 1702) was born in Västerås, Sweden, 100 km west of Stockholm. His father, Johannes Rudbeck, was a Professor of Theology at the University of Uppsala before he became the Bishop of Västerås.

Olof studied for his education at Västerås. He became a scientist, writer and Professor of Medicine at Uppsala University. He also became the first person to write a medical dissertation about the lymph glands. Rudbeck made the first major medical discovery when he discovered the lymphatic system after performing a dissection on a cow carcass in an open market.

The doctor then turned historian and undertook a 30-year endeavour to uncover Sweden's proud origins after noting what he thought were striking similarities between ancient Nordic myths and classical Greek myths. He strongly believed in his extraordinary quest to prove that Sweden was indeed the location of the lost, advanced civilisation Atlantis. Rudbeck began to see connections from classical civilisation to the folklore of Sweden, both in geography and in their legendary rulers. He found ancient inscriptions on stones and he also continued to study the ancient Scandinavian Runes, the tradition of Ragnarok.

In 1675, Rudbeck published *Atlantica*, one of a number of books in which he submitted his strong belief in a Scandinavian Atlantis. He was one of the few writers to suggest that Atlantis was fact, not fiction, and that Scandinavia was one of the first lands occupied by Atlantean survivors.

Anders Celsius

Anders Celsius (27 November 1701 - 25 April 1744) was born in Uppsala, Sweden. He was the son of an astronomy professor and the grandson of a mathematician.

Anders Celsius was an astronomer who invented the Celsius temperature scale, the most widely used in the world today. Celsius was primarily an astronomer and did not even start working on his temperature scale until shortly before his death. He also extended the science of Runes and travelled around the whole of Sweden to examine the *bautastenar megaliths*, which means *'standing stones'*.

Wilhelm Grimm

Wilhelm Carl Grimm also known as Karl (24 February 1786 - 16 December 1859) was a German author. He was born in Hanau,

Germany and in 1803 he started studying law at the University of Marburg.

His older brother was called Jacob Ludwig Carl (1785 - 1863). They are best known as the Brothers Grimm and for their collection of more than 200 fairy and folk tales, such as *Rapunzel, Rumpelstiltskin, The Frog Prince, Hansel and Gretel,* and *Snow White and The Seven Dwarfs.*

Wilhelm Grimm was asked by a friend to investigate the markings on rocks discovered on his estate. This first substantial exploration of the ancient markings made him want to know more and so he began to explore artefacts like helmets, and a book was written on the literature of the Runes. Wilhelm Grimm discussed his findings, the *'Marcomannic Runes'*, in 1821 in *'Ueber Deutsche Runen'*.

It is believed that the Younger Futhark had developed further into the Marcomannic Runes, and then into the Dalecarlian Runes around 1500 to 1800 AD. The origins of the Runic scripts are uncertain.

Heinrich Luitpold Himmler

Heinrich Luitpold Himmler was born in Munich on 7 October 1900 to a Roman Catholic family and died in 1945.

He served in the German army at the end of World War One and then had a variety of jobs, including working as a chicken farmer. He became involved with the Nazi party in the early 1920s and took part in the *'beer hall'* putsch of 1923. Himmler acted as the Nazi party's propaganda leader between 1926 and 1930. In 1929, he was appointed head of the SS and Adolf Hitler's personal bodyguard, and the following year was elected to the Reichstag.

Himmler was to become one of the most feared men once World War Two broke out. Himmler was a keen Astrologist and Cosmologist and became convinced that Germany's future rested in the stars. He was also fascinated by the occult, as were other

Nazi leaders, such as Rudolf Hess. When Heinrich Himmler controlled the German Secret Intelligence Service he set up a special top secret department called the Occult Bureau to gather information on Astrology and the uses of psychic powers in espionage work. He also instigated research into the Runes, in the strong belief that this would further knowledge of a vigorous Germanic culture.

During the Nazi party's rise to power, they embraced symbols from Guido von List's *'Armanen Runes'*. He devoted his life to Runic Occultism and became one of the important figures in Germanic mysticism and runic revivalism in the late 19th and early 20th centuries. He published a book in 1908 called *'Das Geheimnis der Runen'* (The Secret of the Runes), about a set of 18 Armanen Runes, which were based on the Younger Futhark. This followed an 11-month state of temporary blindness after a cataract operation on both eyes in 1902. This vision in 1902 opened up his *'inner eye'* known today as the third eye, and the *'Secret of the Runes'* was revealed to him.

This book highlighted theories of Armanism, a myth of a super race, which he interpreted and considered that the German people belonged to. The book and von List's teachings in general proved to be compelling material for people like Hitler, Goering and Hess, who even became members of his secret Thule Society.

The symbol they used most widely from the Armanen Runes was the Sig Rune, which was repeated as the symbol of Schutz-Staffel (SS), meaning *'protective force'*.

The Schutz-Staffel was a paramilitary Nazi organisation under Adolf Hitler. The SS grew from a small bodyguard unit to a powerful force. In time, it grew into a million men on the front lines, in the concentration camps, in administration and as police.

The Sig Rune ended up being used by Karl Maria Wiligut, who was Himmler's official occultist. The SS Sig Runes design was created in 1931 when Walter Heck, an SS member, drew two reversed and inverted Sig Runes side by side and noticed the similarity to the initials of the SS. Heck sold the rights to the Sig Runes to the SS and the Runes were quickly adopted as the insignia of the Schutz-Staffel. It was turned into a badge and was worn as an armband. It also appeared on weapons and wall slogans.

After the Second World War, the Runes became unpopular because of their association with Nazism.

J.R.R. Tolkien

John Ronald Reuel Tolkien, CBE (3 January 1892 - 2 September 1973) was better known as J.R.R. Tolkien. He was an English writer and poet, and is best known as the author of the classic fantasy novels, *The Hobbit*, *The Lord of the Rings* and *The Silmarillion*.

He used the Anglo-Saxon Runes on a map to highlight its connection to the Dwarves. Runes were also used in the early drafts of *The Lord of the Rings* but he decided to replace them with the 'Cirth'. 'Cirth' was a Rune-like alphabet invented by him and was adapted from the real life Runes.

Today

It was not until the mid-1980s that the New Age movement grew and the Runes regained their popularity as a tool for self-awareness and divination.

They can also be seen in popular culture; for example, Hermione Granger, from the popular *Harry Potter* series by J.K.

Rowling, studies ancient Runes, and the alien Asgard race from the successful American science fiction television series *Stargate SG1* uses Runes as their written language.

Did you know?

The middle name of Bjorn Borg, the former world number one tennis player from Sweden, is '*Rune*'.

Chapter Two

The Rune Poems

An idea can turn to dust or magic,
depending on the talent that rubs against it.
William Bernbach

The Rune Poems are three poems that record the letters of Runic alphabets, while providing a descriptive poetic verse for each letter. The three different poems are the Anglo-Saxon Rune Poem, the Norwegian Rune Poem and the Icelandic Rune Poem.

These ancient poems for Runes were created as an aid for remembering the Rune symbols, names and meanings. Unfortunately, there are no poems existing for the Elder Futhark.

Rune Poems
Anglo-Saxon Rune Poem

The Anglo-Saxon Rune Poem was written in the 8th to 9th centuries. It was preserved in the 10th century manuscript Cotton Otho B.x, fol. 165a - 165b. It is stored at Cotton Library in London.

The Cotton, or Cottonian, Library was privately collected by Sir Robert Bruce Cotton MP (1571 - 1631). Sir Robert collected official records, papers that were poorly kept, and stored them for safe keeping. It is now the basis of the British Library in London.

In 1731, the manuscript was lost in a fire at the Cotton Library. George Hickes, a scholar, had, however, copied the poem in 1705. His copy formed the basis of all later editions of the poem. Many believe that the record of the poem deviated from the original manuscript.

The poem consists of short stanzas, 29 in all, of two to five lines each. At the beginning of each stanza, the Runic characters are described, preceded by their equivalents in ordinary script and followed by their names.

A Copy of the Anglo-Saxon Rune Poem

Source for original text and translation: *Runic and Heroic Poems* by Bruce Dickins, published in 1915.

Old English

Feoh byþ frofur fira gehwylcum; sceal ðeah manna gehwylc miclun hyt dælan

gif he wile for drihtne domes hleotan.

Ur byþ anmod ond oferhyrned, felafrecne deor, feohteþ mid hornum

mære morstapa; þæt is modig wuht.

Þorn byþ ðearle scearp; ðegna gchwylcum anfcng ys yfyl, ungemetum reþe manna gehwelcum, ðe him mid resteð.

Os byþ ordfruma ælere spræce, wisdomes wraþu ond witena frofur

and eorla gehwam eadnys ond tohiht.

Rad byþ on recyde rinca gehwylcum sefte ond swiþhwæt, ðamðe sitteþ on ufan meare mægenheardum ofer milpaþas.

Cen byþ cwicera gehwam, cuþ on fyre blac ond beorhtlic, byrneþ oftust

ðær hi æþelingas inne restaþ.

Gyfu gumcna byþ glcng and hcrenys, wraþu and wyrþscypc and wræcna gehwam ar and ætwist, ðe byþ oþra leas.

Wenne bruceþ, ðe can weana lyt sares and sorge and him sylfa hæfþ blæd and blysse and eac byrga geniht.

Hægl byþ hwitust corna; hwyrft hit of heofones lyfte, wealcaþ hit windes scura; weorþeþ hit to wætere syððan.

Nyd byþ nearu on breostan; weorþeþ hi þeah oft niþa bearnum to helpe and to hæle gehwæþre, gif hi his hlystaþ æror.

Is byþ ofereald, ungemetum slidor, glisnaþ glæshluttur gimmum gelicust, flor forste geworuht, fæger ansyne.

Ger byÞ gumena hiht, ðonne God læteþ, halig heofones cyning, hrusan syllan beorhte bleda beornum ond ðearfum.

Eoh byþ utan unsmeþe treow, heard hrusan fæst, hyrde fyres,wyrtrumun underwreþyd, wyn on eþle.

Peorð byþ symble plega and hlehter wlancum [on middum], ðar wigan sittaþ

on beorsele bliþe ætsomne.

Eolh-secg eard hæfþ oftust on fennewexeð on wature, wundaþ grimme,blode breneð beorna gehwylcne

ðe him ænigne onfeng gedeþ.

Sigel semannum symble biþ on hihte,ðonne hi hine feriaþ ofer fisces beþ,oþ hi brimhengest bringeþ to lande.

Tir biþ tacna sum, healdeð trywa wel wiþ æþelingas; a biþ on færylde ofer nihta genipu, næfre swiceþ.

Beorc byþ bleda leas, bereþ efne swa ðeah tanas butan tudder, biþ on telgum wlitig,heah on helme hrysted fægere,geloden leafum, lyfte getenge.

Eh byþ for eorlum æþelinga wyn,hors hofum wlanc, ðær him hæleþ ymb[e]

welege on wicgum wrixlaþ spræce

and biþ unstyllum æfre frofur.

Man byþ on myrgþe his magan leof:sceal þeah anra gehwylc oðrum swican,forðum drihten wyle dome sine

þæt earme flæsc eorþan betæcan.

Lagu byþ leodum langsum geþuht, gif hi sculun neþan on nacan tealtum

and hi sæyþa swyþe bregaþ and se brimhengest bridles ne gym[eð].

Ing wæs ærest mid East-Denum gesewen secgun, oþ he siððan est

ofer wæg gewat; wæn æfter ran;

ðus Heardingas ðone hæle nemdun.

Eþel byþ oferleof æghwylcum men, gif he mot ðær rihtes and gerysena on

brucan on bolde bleadum oftast.

Dæg byþ drihtnes sond, deore mannum, mære metodes leoht, myrgþ and tohiht eadgum and earmum, eallum brice.

Ac byþ on eorþan elda bearnum flæsces fodor, fereþ gelome ofer ganotes bæþ; garsecg fandaþ

hwæþer ac hæbbe æþele treowe.

Æsc biþ oferheah, eldum dyre stiþ on staþule, stede rihte hylt,ðeah him feohtan on firas monige.

Yr byþ æþelinga and eorla gehwæs wyn and wyrþmynd, byþ on wicge fæger,

fæstlic on færelde, fyrdgcatcwa sum.

Iar byþ eafix and ðeah a bruceþ fodres on foldan, hafaþ fægerne eard

wætre beworpen, ðær he wynnum leofaþ.

Ear byþ egle eorla gehwylcun, ðonn[e] fæstlice flæsc onginneþ,hraw colian, hrusan ceosan blac to gebeddan; bleda gedreosaþ,wynna gewitaþ, wera geswicaþ.

Modern English

Wealth is a comfort to all men; yet must every man bestow it freely, if he wish to gain honour in the sight of the Lord.

The aurochs is proud and has great horns; it is a very savage beast and fights with its horns; a great ranger of the moors, it is a creature of mettle.

The thorn is exceedingly sharp, an evil thing for any knight to touch, uncommonly severe on all who sit among them.

The mouth is the source of all language, a pillar of wisdom and a comfort to wise men,

A blessing and a joy to every knight.

Riding seems easy to every warrior while he is indoors and

very courageous to him who traverses the high-roads on the back of a stout horse.

The torch is known to every living man by its pale, bright flame; it always burns where princes sit within.

Generosity brings credit and honour, which support one's dignity; it furnishes help and subsistence to all broken men who are devoid of aught else.

Bliss he enjoys who knows not suffering, sorrow nor anxiety, and has prosperity and happiness and a good enough house.

Hail is the whitest of grain; it is whirled from the vault of heaven and is tossed about by gusts of wind and then it melts into water.

Trouble is oppressive to the heart; yet often it proves a source of help and salvation to the children of men, to everyone who heeds it betimes.

Ice is very cold and immeasurably slippery; it glistens as clear as glass and most like to gems; it is a floor wrought by the frost, fair to look upon.

Summer is a joy to men, when God, the holy King of Heaven, suffers the earth to bring forth shining fruits for rich and poor alike.

The yew is a tree with rough bark, hard and fast in the earth, supported by its roots,

A guardian of flame and a joy upon an estate.

Peorth is a source of recreation and amusement to the great, where warriors sit blithely together in the banqueting-hall.

The *Eolh*-sedge is mostly to be found in a marsh; it grows in the water and makes a ghastly wound, covering with blood every warrior who touches it.

The sun is ever a joy in the hopes of seafarers when they journey away over the fishes' bath, until the courser of the deep bears them to land.

Tiw is a guiding star; well does it keep faith with princes; it is ever on its course over the mists of night and never fails.

The poplar bears no fruit; yet without seed it brings forth suckers, for it is generated from its leaves. Splendid are its branches and gloriously adorned its lofty crown which reaches to the skies.

The horse is a joy to princes in the presence of warriors. A steed in the pride of its hoofs, when rich men on horseback bandy words about it; and it is ever a source of comfort to the restless.

The joyous man is dear to his kinsmen; yet every man is doomed to fail his fellow,

Since the Lord by his decree will commit the vile carrion to the earth.

The ocean seems interminable to men, if they venture on the rolling bark

and the waves of the sea terrify them

and the courser of the deep heed not its bridle.

Ing was first seen by men among the East-Danes, till, followed by his chariot,

He departed eastwards over the waves.

So the Heardingas named the hero.

An estate is very dear to every man, if he can enjoy there in his house whatever is right and proper in constant prosperity.

Day, the glorious light of the Creator, is sent by the Lord; it is beloved of men, a source of hope and happiness to rich and poor, and of service to all.

The oak fattens the flesh of pigs for the children of men. Often it traverses the gannet's bath, and the ocean proves whether the oak keeps faith in honourable fashion.

The ash is exceedingly high and precious to men. With its sturdy trunk it offers a stubborn resistance, though attacked by many a man.

Yr is a source of joy and honour to every prince and knight; it looks well on a horse and is a reliable equipment for a journey.

Iar is a river fish and yet it always feeds on land; it has a fair abode encompassed by water, where it lives in happiness.

The grave is horrible to every knight, when the corpse quickly begins to cool

and is laid in the bosom of the dark earth.

Prosperity declines, happiness passes away

and covenants are broken.

The Norwegian Rune Poem

The Norwegian Rune Poem has been written down from memory. It is said to be the earliest recorded Rune Poem and the shortest and most simple. It was preserved in a 17th century copy of a destroyed 13th century manuscript, which perished in a fire in 1728 in the University Library at Copenhagen.

It was first printed in Runic characters in *Danica Literatura Antiquissima*, page 105 (Amsterodamiae, 1636) by Olaus Wormius (May 13 1588 - August 31 1655) who was a Danish physician.

This version was used by Vigfusson and Powell in their Icelandic Prose Reader (Oxford, 1879) and *Corpus Poeticum Boreale* (Oxford, 1883).

Later in the seventeenth century, the poem was copied by Árni Magnússon and Jon Eggertsson. It seemed that their transcripts of the poems were far more accurate than Wormius.

The Poem has certain resemblances to the Anglo-Saxon Rune Poem. It is credited to anonymous Norwegian author at the end of the thirteenth century; *ræið* and *rossom* alliterate, which would be impossible with the Icelandic forms of *ræið* and *hrossum*.

The Norwegian Rune Poem consists of sixteen couplets, one for each rune of the younger futhark. All the couplets except two (6 and 15) are in the skaldic metre called *runhent*, characterised by having both alliteration and end-rhyme. The deviations from the metre in stanzas 6 and 15 are probably due to corruption at the oral stage of the tradition.

A Copy of the Norwegian Rune Poem

Source for original text and translation: *Runic and Heroic Poems*
by Bruce Dickins, published in 1915.

Old Norse

Fé vældr frænda róge;
føðesk ulfr í skóge.
Úr er af illu jarne;
opt løypr ræinn á hjarne.
Þurs vældr kvinna kvillu;
kátr værðr fár af illu.
Óss er flæstra færða
fo,r; en skalpr er sværða.
Ræið kveða rossom væsta;
Reginn sló sværðet bæzla.
Kaun er barna bo,lvan;
bo,l gørver nán fo,lvan.
Hagall er kaldastr korna;
Kristr skóp hæimenn forna.
Nauðr gerer næppa koste;
nøktan kælr í froste.
Ís ko,llum brú bræiða;
blindan þarf at læiða.
Ár er gumna góðe;
get ek at o,rr var Fróðe.
Sól er landa ljóme;
lúti ek helgum dóme.
Týr er æinendr ása;
opt værðr smiðr blása.
Bjarkan er laufgrønstr líma;
Loki bar flærða tíma.
Maðr er moldar auki;
mikil er græip á hauki.
Lo,gr er, fællr ór fjalle

foss; en gull ero nosser.

Ýr er vetrgrønstr viða;

vænt er, er brennr, at sviða.

Modern English

Wealth is a source of discord among kinsmen;

the wolf lives in the forest.

Dross comes from bad iron;

the reindeer often races over the frozen snow.

Giant causes anguish to women;

misfortune makes few men cheerful.

Estuary is the way of most journeys;

but a scabbard is of swords.

Riding is said to be the worst thing for horses;

Reginn forged the finest sword.

Ulcer is fatal to children;

death makes a corpse pale.

Hail is the coldest of grain;

Christ created the world of old.

Constraint gives scant choice;

a naked man is chilled by the frost.

Ice we call the broad bridge;

the blind man must be led.

Plenty is a boon to men;

I say that Frothi was generous.

Sun is the light of the world;

I bow to the divine decree.

Tyr is a one-handed god;

often has the smith to blow.

Birch has the greenest leaves of any shrub;

Loki was fortunate in his deceit.

Man is an augmentation of the dust;

great is the claw of the hawk.

A waterfall is a River which falls from a mountain-side;

but ornaments are of gold.
Yew is the greenest of trees in winter;
it is wont to crackle when it burns.

The Icelandic Rune Poem

This Rune Poem has been dated from the 11th to 15th centuries. The Icelandic Rune Poem is recorded in four Arnamagnæan Manuscripts. The youngest of the four documents dates from the late 15th century. Arnamagnæan derives its name from the Icelandic scholar, Árni Magnússon (13 November 1663 - 7 January 1730), as he assembled the manuscript collection.

The poem consists of 16 short stanzas dealing in succession with the letter names of the Scandinavian Runic alphabet. Each stanza contains three *kenningar* – the elaborate periphrases, which are commonly found in Icelandic literature.

Old Norse

Fé er frænda róg
ok flæðar viti
ok grafseiðs gata
aurum fylkir.
Úr er skýja grátr
ok skára þverrir
ok hirðis hatr.
umbre vísi
Þurs er kvenna kvöl
ok kletta búi
ok varðrúnar verr.
Saturnus þengill.
Óss er algingautr
ok ásgarðs jöfurr,
ok valhallar vísi.
Jupiter oddviti.
Reið er sitjandi sæla

ok snúðig ferð
ok jórs erfiði.
iter ræsir.
Kaun er barna böl
ok bardaga [för]
ok holdfúa hús.
flagella konungr.
Hagall er kaldakorn
ok krapadrífa
ok snáka sótt.
grando hildingr.
Nauð er Þýjar þrá
ok þungr kostr
ok vássamlig verk.
opera niflungr.
Íss er árbörkr
ok unnar þak
ok feigra manna fár.
glacies jöfurr.
Ár er gumna góði
ok gott sumar
algróinn akr.
annus allvaldr.
Sól er skýja skjöldr
ok skínandi röðull
ok ísa aldrtregi.
rota siklingr.
Týr er einhendr áss
ok ulfs leifar
ok hofa hilmir.
Mars tiggi.
Bjarkan er laufgat lim
ok lítit tré
ok ungsamligr viðr.

abies buðlungr.
Maðr er manns gaman
ok moldar auki
ok skipa skreytir.
homo mildingr.
Lögr er vellanda vatn
ok viðr ketill
ok glömmungr grund.
lacus lofðungr.
Ýr er bendr bogi
ok brotgjarnt járn
ok fífu fárbauti.
arcus ynglingr.

Modern English

Wealth
source of discord among kinsmen
and fire of the sea
and path of the serpent.
Shower
lamentation of the clouds
and ruin of the hay-harvest
and abomination of the shepherd.
Giant
torturer of women
and cliff-dweller
and husband of a giantess.
God
aged Gautr
and prince of Ásgarðr
and lord of Vallhalla.
Riding
joy of the horsemen
and speedy journey

and toil of the steed.
Ulcer
disease fatal to children
and painful spot
and abode of mortification.
Hail
cold grain
and shower of sleet
and sickness of serpents.
˟Constraint
grief of the bond-maid
and state of oppression
and toilsome work.
Ice
bark of rivers
and roof of the wave
and destruction of the doomed.
Plenty
boon to men
and good summer
and thriving crops.
Sun
shield of the clouds
and shining ray
and destroyer of ice.
Týr
god with one hand
and leavings of the wolf
and prince of temples.
Birch
leafy twig
and little tree
and fresh young shrub.
Man

delight of man
and augmentation of the earth
and adorner of ships.
Water
eddying stream
and broad geysir
and land of the fish.
Yew
bent bow
and brittle iron
and giant of the arrow.

Chapter Three

Casting the Runes

That's the thing with magic.
You've got to know it's still here,
all around us, or it just stays invisible for you.
Charles de Lint

Any of the books you will read will provide you with several different ways to read Runes. What works for one may not work for another. For example, some students have found it difficult to do an in-depth reading, as it makes no sense to them, yet others have found learning the Runes straightforward and face no problems.

There are no rules for casting the Runes and it is a very personal thing. Finding your own method of casting is the best way forward. When you are casting the Runes for yourself, finding a quiet time and place, where the distractions of everyday life do not intrude, will help you to focus your energies on the reading.

Clear your mind and direct your consciousness to the casting of the Runes. If you have a specific question you wish to ask, clearly formulate that question in your mind. Close your eyes; relax; take time and then reach into the pouch and draw the Rune(s). In interpreting the Runes that you have drawn, it is important that you consider the overall spread and the relationship of the Runes to each other, as well as individually.

In your Rune journal, you can note down your question and record what Rune you have chosen. Before you begin to do casting for friends and family, you may like to draw out one Rune each day. How you can do this is explained below.

You may decide to make your own Runes. If so, you can buy

your Rune casting cloth from New Age shops or the internet. Or you can make your own Runes as suggested in Chapter Seven.

Before the Rune Reading

Lay down your Rune cloth for your reading. Place your hand over the bag of Runes, slowly sweep your hand over it and you may feel a tingling feeling in the palm of your hand. Place your hand into the Rune pouch, swirl the Runes around in the bag gently with your hand, and let the Runes fall naturally into your fingers; sense whether it is the right one to draw. Slowly draw out the Runes and gently throw them on the cloth. Read the Runes in the order that they were placed on the cloth.

One Rune Casting – The Single Rune – Odin's Rune

The single Rune reading is known as Odin's Rune, but some of my students call casting a single Rune 'the day Rune'. This is a good way for you to get an answer to a single question quickly and simply. You can do this either in the morning to shed light on the coming day or in the evening for reflection on the day you have encountered.

Drawing one Rune will provide you with an overview of a situation, and this will help you to gain focus on the presenting issue and provide you with a fresh perspective. A daily Rune draw is a very good way to learn. You might want to start with whichever Rune you feel drawn to. Then, stay with that Rune until you feel ready to move onto the next. You might stay with the first Rune for one day or maybe even a week. From student experiences, if you draw a new Rune each day, you might not be quite ready to move on, so feel free to take your time.

Casting a single Rune to celebrate significant events in your life, such as birthdays, New Year, Solstices, Equinoxes, even the passing of a relative or friend, can aid your spiritual journey.

The Three Norns – Three Rune Casting

A Norns casting is very simple to do. It is called Norns because of the three Goddesses, which are sometimes called the Weird Sisters. They are spinners of destiny, symbolising past, present and future. Urd is the first Goddess and represents the past, or what has been. Verdandi is the second Goddess and represents the ever-changing present, or what is. The third Goddess, Skuld, oversees all that is yet unresolved and which determines the future or what shall be.

The Norn Spread is used to interpret a situation over time. You read the Runes from left to right. The first Rune represents the past of the situation in question. The second indicates the present, the path that the client is currently on. The third suggests the future, a likely outcome if one continues on the present path.

Five Rune Spread

The Five Rune Spread can give you detailed overviews on your current life direction, how you will achieve your goals, and the lessons you are learning.

In a spread, the sequence in which Runes are drawn determines their position and significance. Each place in a Rune

casting has a meaning attached to it.

The first Rune represents an overview of your current life. The second Rune represents the challenges you may face. The third Rune represents the course of action called for. The fourth Rune drawn is the obstacle, surrender or sacrifice that you may have to face. The fifth Rune drawn is the new situation or opportunity that is coming to you.

Six Rune Spread – Runic Cross

Draw six Runes of your choice and place them in the following order:

Place the first Rune in the centre to represent you now.

The second Rune goes to the right of the first Rune and represents the past.

The third Rune goes to the right of the first Rune and represents the future. The fourth Rune is placed below the first Rune and reveals the situation you are currently in.

The fifth Rune is placed above the first Rune and this indicates the challenge ahead.

The sixth Rune goes above the fifth Rune and represents the best outcome.

Casting Runes for the Forthcoming Year

Thirteen Runes are needed for this yearly spread. You may, if you wish, start with the month you are currently in, or begin with January.

The chosen thirteen Runes represent the months of the year. Place them in front of you in a clockwise direction.

The thirteenth Rune is to be placed in the middle and represents ourselves and what our influences may be for the coming year.

Casting Runes on the Sabbats

The Sabbats are celebrations for Pagans and Wiccans. The Sabbats mark the changing season in the passing of the year, which are represented on the Wheel of the Year. Each Sabbat represents a different aspect of life. They are based on Celtic religious festivals and there are eight Sabbats.

The first Sabbat, which is the Pagan/Wiccan New Year and last harvest of the old year, is Samhain which falls on Halloween, October 31st. The name '*Samhain*' is derived from Old Irish and means '*Summer's End*'. It is believed at this time that the veil between our world and the spirit world is the thinnest, allowing spirits to walk amongst us.

The next Sabbat is Yule, which falls on the Winter Solstice, December 21st, and marks the first day of the season of winter. It is a celebration of the shortest day and longest night of the year, when the sun is at the greatest distance from the equator. Some Pagans and Wiccans see it as New Year's Day and burn a traditional Yule log to give the sun strength.

The next Sabbat is Imbolc, which is celebrated on February 2nd and is regarded as the first day of spring, when life begins to stir again. Imbolc is derived from Old Irish '*i mbolg*', which means '*in the belly*' and refers to ewes' pregnancies. This is a good time for us to clear out old clutter and make way for new growth.

Eostre/Ostara is the next Sabbat, which falls on the Vernal Spring Equinox, March 21st, and marks the first day of spring. The name Eostre/Ostara is derived from the German Goddess of fertility and new beginnings. This is a day of sowing the crops to ensure that there is a harvest in autumn. From this point on, there will be more hours of daylight than there are of night.

Next is Beltane, which falls on May Day and is the last of the three spring festivals. Beltane is derived from the Irish Gaelic word '*Bealtaine*', meaning '*bright/sacred fire*'. Beltane is celebrated with maypole dances, symbolising the celebration of spring and the flowering of life. Bonfires are lit for purification and transition, heralding in the season in the hope of a good harvest later in the year

Litha is the next Sabbat, which falls on the Summer Solstice, June 21st. This is a significant point in the Wheel of the Year, as it is a time to celebrate growth and life and see balance in the world. The shifting of the yearly seasons is acknowledged as the sun will not begin to decline once more towards winter.

The turning of the Wheel of the Year brings us to Lammas/Lughnasadh (pronounced *loo'nass'ah*), which is on August 1st. It is a festival celebrating the beginning of the harvest. It is named to honour the Celtic god, Lugh, whose name means '*light*' or '*shining*'. Lughnasadh is the first of the three harvest Sabbats; Mabon and Samhain being the other two, which celebrate the ripening grains and corn. This Sabbat is also known as the celebration of bread. As bread was one of the main staples of our ancestors, the ripening of the grain was cause for great celebration.

The last Sabbat is Mabon, which falls on the Autumn Equinox, September 21st. It is a celebration of the second harvest, and also when day and night are of equal duration before we descend into the final festival. For many, it is now time to reflect on the past year on our achievements. Our ancestors held this festival to give thanks to the Goddess for giving the community enough food to last the winter months.

Choosing the Runes

You may wish to choose eight Runes at the beginning of Samhain or on each day of the Sabbat. Each Rune chosen represents a Sabbat, and each Sabbat represents the timeline of the forecasting of the Runes. Write the Runes down in the order they were drawn. Then interpret the Runes, separately and as a whole.

Other Ideas
Creative Writing – Rune Journal

Keeping a special Rune journal for your readings can be of great assistance as you get to know the Runes. Keeping track of your readings and thoughts will help strengthen your intuition and connection with the Runes.

At Home

Some of my students paint the Rune symbols on large stones and place them in their garden. Others have painted their favourite Rune stones on kitchen and bathroom tiles.

Chapter Four

The Meanings of the Runes

The power of Thought, the magic of the Mind!
Lord Byron

Rune Meanings

Runemasters or Runecarvers were specialists in making Rune stones. During ancient times, many stones were carved out from a flat piece of rock. Wood and leather were also used.

Our ancestors believed that stones were alive and had a soul and a spirit. They held the idea that each stone had much wisdom, magic and lessons to teach them in their daily lives.

THE AETTS

The Runes are divided into three groups or rows of eight called *aettir*. This reflects the ancient mystical numerological tradition of Northern Europe as eight was a number with great power and significance to the Vikings. The English word *'eight'* is derived from the Nordic word *'aett'*, which means eight.

THE FIRST AETT

The first Aett is *Frey's Aett*. The first eight runes are associated with the fertility Goddess Frey/Freyr/Freyia. They are associated with the creation of the world, its inhabitants and the beings that reside upon it. The Runes in this Aett deal with the basics of life, the things we own that help us live our lives, our knowledge, pleasures we desire and how we interact with all the people and all of the things within our lives. This Aett is named after Freya, because the first Rune in it is said to have been derived from the name Freya. It consists of the following Runes: Fehu, Uruz, Thurisaz, Ansuz, Raidho, Kenaz, Gebo and Wunjo.

THE SECOND AETT

The second Aett is named after Heimdall/Hagal/Hel/Hagall, the elemental force of hail and storm. The Runes in the second Aett deal with the natural forces of our world and universe, those we have no control over, such as time, our spiritual growth and personal evolution. It is also connected with achievements, opportunities and successes. This Aett is named after the God Hagal, after whom the first Rune of this Aett is named. It consists of the following Runes: Hagalaz, Naudhiz, Isa, Jera, Eihwaz, Pertho, Elhaz and Sowilo.

THE THIRD AETT

The third Aett is called Tyr and is associated with the God of war and justice, Tyr. He was also a Sky God whose worship went back to the Bronze Age. The third Aett is associated with those experiences which mould and transform our lives. It is also connected to human conditioning, social aspects and our spiritual transformation, attainment and growth. This Aett is named after the God Tyr, because the first Rune in this Aett (Teiwaz) is named Tyr. It consists of the following Runes: Teiwaz, Berkana, Elhaz, Mannaz, Laguz, Inguz, Dagaz and Othila.

Each Rune has a unique vibration and energy. It can therefore provide us with a better understanding of our pathway in life and assist us in gaining a better understanding of ourselves and others.

The first step in learning to read the Runes is to get to know the Runes themselves. You do not need to memorise each interpretation, as this may hinder your intuition. Our attitudes, beliefs and feelings shape our future for either success or failure.

Negative thoughts translate into giving up the incentive to learn the Runes. Our fears could simply be a state of our minds based on past experiences and the anticipation grows because we may not know the future outcome. When we hold onto fear, however, we are actually stopping ourselves from reaching our highest potential. Taking baby steps rather than giant ones will assist you to devise your own method in learning this ancient art form.

Learning the Runes does take time and it will not happen overnight. Our fears do run rampant due to the lack of trust we may have in ourselves in learning something new. As Franklin D. Roosevelt once said, *'There is nothing to fear but fear itself.'* Remember that fears are learned beliefs. Maybe try and keep your mind and energy in the present moment and trust your intuition.

Rune Journal Meditation

I always keep a record of what Rune readings I carry out in a journal. Doing this may help you also to think about each individual Rune and its context in the reading you are doing for yourself, family and friends.

When you are ready, another starting point for you to do on a daily basis is to meditate on each Rune, beginning with Fehu and ending with Othala. This serves as a dual purpose, as it will expand your understanding of the meanings on a conscious and unconscious level. This exercise can also be used for self-empowerment, and as you connect to the Rune energies they become available to you when they are needed. According to your need at that moment in time, you may be able to visualise them on their own or in groups and connect with their energies to empower you on a daily basis. Your connection to the Runes will become deeper, more personal and more profound as you meditate; this will give you a true understanding of what each Rune means.

The First Aett – Freya

Fehu

Pronounced:	fay-hu
Astrological:	Aries/ Taurus
Tarot:	Tower
Element:	Fire/ Earth
Key Words:	Harmony, Fertility, Wealth

Fehu is the first Rune of the first Aett, and is associated and sacred to the Goddess Frey and Freyja. In Norse mythology, Freya is portrayed as a Goddess of love, beauty and fertility. Blonde, blue-eyed and beautiful, Freya is described as the fairest of all goddesses, and people prayed to her for happiness in love. She was also called on to assist childbirths and prayed to for good seasons.

The meaning of the word *'Fehu'* is *'Cattle'*, and derives from the Germanic root-word *'vieh'*. A Norse myth tells of Auðhumla, the primal cow that was formed at the beginning of the world from melting ice. Four streams of milk poured from her udder and Auðhumla licked salty ice; from the ice block appeared the first human being. Our ancient ancestors believed that owning cattle meant wealth, as they could sell and trade their cattle, which resulted in their wealth increasing. Cattle were the principal source of food and clothing for them and they used their horns as drinking cups.

The upward thrusting staves of this Rune represent the horns of the cow. The original Rune's meaning of *'money, cattle* and *wealth'* can be linked today with material wealth and possessions. It also signifies a time when you may feel a strong need to understand your thoughts and feelings, and this is a great opportunity to get to know your true self better. This Rune can also indicate that you are entering a period of personal and spiritual growth. Seeking times of solitude may be required for you to connect with your inner self.

As the Fehu Rune is associated with the Goddess Freya who governs fertility, this Rune can mean the conception and birth of a creative idea or enterprise.

This is a great Rune to draw, as it reminds us not to be greedy or selfish with our good fortune.

Achievement and recognition through hard and determined work is also associated with the Fehu Rune and can indicate possible pay rises, promotions or career advancement.

The symbol Fehu can be drawn on paper to attract abundance. Keeping Fehu inside your pocket, wallet or purse will attract money. Why not draw and use this symbol for the realisation of hard work on a business project or venture as it draws to an end. As it is something you have worked hard for, you can see what you have achieved.

I use this Rune to advance projects and goals to the next stage, and to protect my property and valuables. I also use it to give my career an added boost, and to increase wealth. Repeated use of the Rune Fehu can increase confidence in self-empowerment and the ability to provide for oneself. Using Fehu as a divination tool for personal and spiritual development can assist you with confidence in other areas of life including work, creative pursuits, family and work relationships.

Overall, the appearance of the Fehu Rune is seen as a very welcome one that promises abundance, health, wealth and happiness.

Uruz

Pronounced: oo-rooz
Key Words: Power, Energy
Astrological: Taurus/Leo
Tarot: High Priestess
Element: Earth
Key Words: Freedom, Healing, Health, Vitality,
                     Strength, Power, Gratitude, Courage,
                     Change

This is the second Rune in the first Aett. It represents the European wild ox, the aurochs, similar to a longhorn bull, that was once found all over Europe. These wild untameable cattle of Northern Europe became extinct in the 17th century.

Aurochs were reputed to have had horns as long as six feet, which were highly prized by people as drinking horns.

Paintings of aurochs have been found in Neolithic caves, and it was believed that the hunting of the aurochs was seen as a *'rite of passage'* for boys entering manhood. The ancient people of the Norse saw the horn of the aurochs as a symbol of strength. It was used to swear oaths upon, make firm friendships by and to clinch deals.

When we choose this Rune, it enables us to find the inner strength to fulfil our dreams. This strength is not a force to wield over others, but it does not allow others to exert their power over you. In using your inner strength, you are able to keep focused on the path you are travelling without being outmanoeuvred.

This Rune can give us great strength in looking at the birth of new beginnings. Everything will work itself out; having inner belief that it will be OK is the key.

Rewards are also possible and there could be a strong indication that the life you have been living has in some way outgrown its form and must change, so new ideas and new life can come forward.

Uruz is the Rune of harmony, order and inner strength. It often marks the end of something and the start of new beginnings in our lives. This may be a sign for you to take the time to shake off the past and to take advantage of new opportunities. Remember, before each new beginning must come an ending, and endings can be emotional; but know deep down that you will ultimately benefit from these experiences.

Uruz also aids your inner strength as you begin to tackle these new challenges. Persistence is worthwhile in creative projects. You may feel that you cannot think clearly in deciding what path to follow, as you may be bombarded by experiencing lack of clarity in thought. Using the mantra, 'Don't stop believing, this soon will pass', will help you in periods of self-doubt.

When this symbol is drawn on a piece of paper, it can boost our energy levels. It acts like a light switch that has the intention of instantly boosting your vigour.

Draw or visualise the Rune symbol in front of you. It can be used any time, especially when you are feeling low on energy, as your strengths and weakness may become imbalanced.

We can use the energy of this Rune to revisit our goals and accomplishments. Set and visualize your goals, write down what you would like to achieve, so that you always have a clear view in mind of where you are now, and which direction you are going. Create action plans so that you can turn your goals into reality by defining what needs to be done to move forward.

Thurisaz

Pronounced: thur-ee-sahz
Astrological: Leo
Tarot   The Emperor
Element: Fire
Key Words: Strength, Good News, Protection

Thurisaz is the third Rune in the first Aett. Thurisaz is a very ancient name for Thor. Thor is the God of thunder, son of Odin. Thor's wife is Sif, and the English fifth day of the week is named Thursday after Thor.

Thor owned a short hammer, called *Mjöllnir*, and when it was thrown at a target, it would return magically to him. It was common for the ancient Norse to wear a small hammer around their neck to invoke Thor's protective powers. Many believe that Thurisaz has been designed to depict Thor's hammer.

The original Norse meaning of the word '*Thurisaz*' is '*Frost Giant*'. When this is translated, it means *giant, monster, demon* or *devil*. The Frost Giants were enemies of the Gods and they all lived in fear of Thor who was the only God who could kill them.

In the Anglo-Saxon Futhorc, this Rune was called Thorn. This may have had different meanings at that moment in time, but Thurisaz has been described as a thorn as many believe it is shaped like one. In ancient times, thorny bushes were used to fence and protect boundaries, and one form of Norse execution was to throw criminals into thorns.

When we choose this Rune, we may be presented with new possibilities that we may not be able to face at that moment in time. You may need to seek counsel before making decisions, as this is now not the time to make hasty decisions.

This Rune may indicate you facing aggression in resolving ongoing problems. You may feel that you will have to stand your ground in order for your point of view to be heard. It may also indicate upheavals in our relationships.

Thurisaz is a symbol of protection and you will feel protected when you cast this Rune. There is a strong element of luck associated with this Rune and this may be presented in various ways unknown to you.

As Thurisaz was called Thorn in Anglo-Saxon times, this could represent the thorn as the obstacle we are facing at this moment in time. As this Rune can act as a shield, it allows us to have faith in ourselves as we face what is in front of us.

You can draw the symbol of Thurisaz and use it for protection for you and your family.

Ansuz

Pronounced: ahn-sooz
Astrological: Leo/Virgo
Tarot: Death
Element: Air
Key Words: Communication, Divine Inspiration,
             Spiritual Power, Wisdom, Ideas,
             knowledge

The fourth Rune of the first Aett is Ansuz. Ansuz is primarily known as Odin's Rune. Ansur represents the ash tree, Yggdrasil, the World Tree from which Odin hung to gain Runic knowledge to convey to mankind. In Nordic mythology, the ash tree recurs in many myths, which tell of its branches and roots holding all the nine worlds together: Asgard, Home of the Gods; Alfheim; Vanaheim, Home of the Vanas; Midgard, Middle Earth; Jotunheim, Home of the Giants; Svartalfheim; Niflheim, Home of the Dead; Muspellsheim, Home of Fire; and Helheim, the Underworld.

The ancient meaning of the Ansuz Rune is *'messenger'*. Ancient Norse storytellers would trek from villages to towns and sit by the campfire to tell stories of the old way of life. *What stories do you have to tell that can inspire others?*

Ansuz can give us insight into our problems and the inspiration and enthusiasm to speak your *'truth'*. This Rune governs communication of all kinds, standing in integrity with yourself and speaking your truth, even when it isn't easy. It may feel scary to speak your truth, especially when you are expressing your values, beliefs, needs and desires, but it is so important. If you hold back, it will become a disservice to yourself and to those with whom you have relationships.

Ansuz can also assist us to connect with our own inner wisdom and knowledge. It helps us to contain our own light and strength as we create our own realities. This Rune reminds us that our thoughts determine what reality we create in our lives. It's all about *our* choices – how and what we choose, upon what we focus, concentrate or direct our attention, and where we spend our mental and emotional energies; this is precisely what we will attract or draw to ourselves. And the universe *always* provides.

Ansuz can also represent a spiritual teacher or leader who can help us connect with our spiritual selves. They may act as a guide as we embark on a spiritual and emotional journey. This may also be a good time to take time out to reflect on your spiritual journey, as every individual will experience their own spiritual journey in a personal way.

If you are experiencing a lack of clarity or even a misunderstanding, you may wish to draw Ansuz on a piece of card. When this Rune is drawn, it gives us the confidence to deal with any kind of lack of communication.

Raidho

Pronounced: rah-eed-ho
Astrological: Sagittarius/Virgo
Tarot: The Hierophant
Element: Air
Key Words: Journey, Pilgrimage, Change, Action,
                  Cartwheel

Raidho is the fifth rune of the first Aett and is known as the travellers' Rune. This Rune has a variety of meanings and has been interpreted as *'Journey'*, *'Wheel'*, *'Wagon'*, *'Chariot'* and *'Riding'*. This is because of the Nordic people travelling in horse-drawn wagons carrying their goods to market.

Raidho represents the overall journey of our lives. Some may call it destiny or fate; others would say it is about life lessons. Norse mythology tells the tale of our course of life being determined by three weaving sisters called the *'Norns'*. The three sisters would weave the fates of all mankind. The first sister, Urd (*'becoming'*), spins the yarn of each individual's fate. The second, Verdandi (*'being'*), measures the yarn. The third, Skuld (*'that to come'*), cuts the yarn.

This Rune also represents the road we are travelling on in life and shows us the way forward. What is the road that you are driving on like? Is the road that you are travelling on bumpy, slippery or winding? This may represent the way that you are currently feeling. Whether it is a physical, emotional, mental or spiritual journey, this Rune will help us to gain a perspective on our travels, which may lead to spiritual transformation. So, if you are feeling out of sync and Raidho is cast in your reading, it will help you to recognise in which direction your daily life is going.

Raidho helps us to be in the right place at the right time; this is called 'Universal Timing'. They say that everything happens for a reason, but sometimes we may feel that the universal idea of what constitutes a 'reason' doesn't quite agree with ours. We may be faced with the same life lessons, because for some reason we may not have recognised the message that we need to learn in order to evolve. Many times, we attract the same type of lesson over and over again because of our unconscious need to work out past emotional issues. Each life lesson that we come across serves as a mirror, a reflection of the energy we emit into the world. So, the question that we can ask ourselves is, what can I do to change the energy that I put out into the world, so that I can attract the right people and circumstances that match my true goals and true self?

When we are feeling unsure about what decisions need to be made, this Rune may tell us that there are going to be delays and possibly difficult journeys. It can also mean that there are important life lessons that need to be learned.

This Rune has also been connected to the Wheel of the Year: The Eight Pagan/ Wiccan Sabbats. The reason for this is because, if we were to draw a circle and make eight lines all intersecting in the centre, it would look similar to a wagon wheel, and each point on this circle represents the seasons as they pass. You may wish to draw the Wheel of the Year to help you recognise what goals you would like to achieve during the changing seasons of the year. From my own experience, this allows me to channel my creative energies in effective ways, allowing me to accomplish my goals.

Kenaz

Pronounced: ken-ahz
Astrological: Cancer/Taurus/Virgo/Libra
Tarot: The Chariot
Element: Water/Fire
Key Words: Vision, Revelation, Knowledge,
                 Creativity

Kenaz is the sixth Rune of the first Aett. The name of this Rune is derived from *'kernan'*, the ancient Germanic word for *'knowing'*, and is translated as *'Torch'*.

In the Anglo-Saxon poem, it says of Kenaz that *'the torch is living fire bright and shining, most often it burns when noble people are at rest indoors'*.

Kenaz supports us by finding the light within us when we are feeling down about life and feel that nothing is going right for us, no matter what we try and do. It helps us to find the *'fire in our bellies'*, and helps overcome stagnation. It helps us to burn and fan the flames of fire through self-doubt. It acts like a conduit for acting on what makes us feel alive.

This Rune has also been known as the Rune of knowledge, teaching and learning.

When this Rune is cast in our readings, it brings about radical and permanent change in our lives in every area possible. It could also mean our way of thinking will be changed, as Kenaz indicates craftsmanship and skill, and supports us to look at our creative abilities; it can give birth to a new idea for a creative project such as a novel, a piece of art or making jewellery, etc. It gives us the drive behind the creation of the projects to the very end.

Kenaz can also be used for self-empowerment. This Rune encourages us to let go of what is no longer serving us for our highest good. Listen intuitively to your feelings in moving forward with your life and also learning when to surrender to what you really do not need to have in your life.

If you are a writer like me, you may experience writer's block. If you are feeling frustrated, just breathe; you can get through it and say as a mantra, 'This soon will pass.' To help fuel your writing again, simply draw this Rune on pieces of card. I leave them in several notebooks around the home. As I always carry a notebook with me to jot down my ideas, I have drawn the Kenaz Rune in the pages. After I have drawn this Rune, I give it time and I send out a clear intention of what I would like to create and then I do 'Free Writing'. I sit down and write anything and everything for a period of ten minutes to start. Don't stop, no matter what. Keep writing, even if you think what you're typing is gibberish, full of misspellings and grammatically wrong; don't worry; get your hand moving, your heart racing and your brain will think it's writing. This Rune symbol can also be drawn on pieces of coloured card to ignite new ideas and to complete unfinished projects.

Gebo

Pronounced: gheb-o
Astrological: Virgo/Libra/Pisces
Tarot   The Lovers
Element: Air/Water
Key Words: Gift, Talent, Freedom, Relationships

Gebo is the seventh Rune of the first Aett. Gebo is connected to the Norse/Germanic Goddess Gefn, 'The Bountiful Giver', Goddess of good fortune. She is also known as a seer and the Goddess of virtue. Stories were told that if a woman died as a virgin, she would be sent to her and she would be looked after in the afterlife.

The number seven is considered lucky by many different cultures. The main reason is because the world was created in six days; the seventh day became a rest day, a special day for Hebrews, the Sabbath. As time passed, the ancient people began to associate the number seven with good luck and being blessed in a special way.

The X symbol inscribed on this Rune represents a sacred mark, indicating the connection between man and the Gods. Ancient people would bring gifts and make sacrifices to their Gods hoping they would have a good harvest to see them through the winter months. Norse myths implied that when a gift was given, another one needed to be returned, which placed the giver under obligation. Gift giving was considered a contract that was binding until an exchange was made. Today, Gebo is more about exchange and contracts than an actual gift. Our Norse ancestors, however, believed that it has no meaning at all because it cannot be reversed.

The Gebo Rune is seen as extremely lucky in a casting. It foretells that a gift/blessing will bestowed upon you. Gebo can be used to empower all our relationships, whether personal or business. Gebo is a positive Rune and it also reminds us of what our talents and skills are. It is time to use those gifts to their full potential and search for new possibilities that will open new doors for us.

Today, the Gebo symbol is commonly used beneath signatures on cards that we send to families and friends to represent a kiss, the symbol of affection.

If you wish to increase your abundance, you may want to draw this symbol to attract more prosperity into your life. If you have an interview, exam or audition coming up, *why not draw this symbol on a piece of card and take it with you?* You may also be able to draw the symbol in your mind's eye before you go into the room, as it will help you feel much more at ease.

Wunjo

Pronounced: woon-yo
Astrological: Libra/Scorpio/Leo
Tarot: Strength
Element: Earth
Key Words: Joy, Bliss, Happiness, Good News,
                Harmony

Wunjo is the eighth and final Rune of the first Aett. The meaning of Wunjo is joy. The symbol is based on the shape of a traditional Scandinavian weathervane.

The oldest translated word for Wunjo is *'perfection'*. There is a term in Anglo-Saxon, *'wuldortanas'*, which means *'glory twigs'*. Many Rune scholars and historians have associated them with the Wunjo Rune. The Anglo-Saxon word is *'Wynn'*, which in modern English is the word *'winning'*. *'Wynn'* meant *'peaceful'* in the Anglo-Saxon definition.

In old German, the word *'Wish'* or *'Wunsch'* means wellbeing/blessed. In the Anglo-Saxon Rune Poem, it is said of Wunjo that *'Joy is for one who knows little of woe, pains and sorrows, and to him who has power and bliss and buildings good enough'*. The Norse people believed that part of this joy came from personal gifts from their God, Odin. Odin was also known as the Wish-Father and was a granter of wishes and prosperity. He carried a *'wishing-rod'* that gave emotional and physical blessings to his followers.

In a casting, Wunjo indicates the end of one cycle and the preparation of the next one at the same time. It is a positive time, as we learn more about life lessons on our spiritual journey. It is a time for recharging our batteries for the next steps ahead.

When we cast this Rune in a reading, it indicates that new beginnings will begin to flourish. Wunjo also brings comfort, joy and pleasure, along with prosperity and harmony.

When we choose Wunjo as a single Rune, it gives us time to reflect on the path we have already taken, and contemplate how far we have travelled and what we have accomplished. We can then make choices and preparations for the future.

If you feel that you have had a tough time lately, Wunjo reminds us of the hope and joy we have achieved by overcoming problems. You may be feeling out of sync because you are experiencing an emotionally challenging time, which is bringing you unhappiness and draining your energy. To resolve this issue, you may want to put your energy into positive situations, which will return that energy and bring you joy.

You may want to hold back on starting new ventures, as communication may be misunderstood. Accomplishing anything seems a hard task as you feel you are being delayed and pulled in different directions.

If you are faced with troubling times, drawing the Wunjo symbol on a piece of coloured card helps you to find a positive outcome.

The Second Aett – Heimdall/Hagal/Hel

Hagalaz

Pronounced:	ha-ga-lahz
Astrological:	Taurus/Scorpio/ Aquarius
Tarot:	The World
Element:	Earth/Water
Key Words:	Disruption, Interference, Change

Hagalaz is the ninth Rune and the first Rune of the second Aett.

The word Hagalaz means 'Hail' or 'Hailstone.' Hagalaz is known as the Rune of the unconscious mind.

The number nine is a sacred number in Norse mythology, as there are nine homeworlds amalgamated by the World Tree, Yggdrasil. Odin also hung upside down on the giant ash tree for nine days and nights to gain insight into the Rune symbols.

When this Rune is cast, it reminds us that we must let go of the past. It is only when we let go of emotional blocks and ties to the past that we can truly move forward. Yet frozen by our fears, we tend to feel that we cannot think straight, which often keeps us from enjoying the freedom that is naturally ours. When we do this, it prevents future spiritual growth and moving forward. It is also important that we gain knowledge from the lesson so that history does not repeat itself and we find ourselves learning from it again. Opportunities will present themselves in better circumstances.

Hagalaz alerts us to be awake, aware and to pay attention to what messages we are sending out into the world. It also acts as a reminder that the universe will always send you signs to help you through whatever you're dealing with. It also helps us to become tuned in to these messages, this communication from the universe directly to you. It acts as a reminder that you are guided in every moment of your life and you are not alone.

This Rune shakes things up in our lives. The way we perceive events that unfold may come as a shock/surprise to us. This may indicate setbacks but it is happening for a reason. Situations may seem out of control, but you may feel a sudden rush of empowerment that enables you to get through your predicament.

If you are familiar with Tarot, you will understand that many people regard the Tower as a negative card. This Rune is sometimes viewed in the same way. However, this Rune can only be unconstructive if we choose it to be. If we decline to learn the lessons that it can teach us, then we will find ourselves back at square one. The concept of 'out with the old, in with the new' is necessary for our spiritual growth and advancement to take place.

You may be faced with recurring challenges in your life. If you embrace these rather than fear them, they will not be so daunting and scary as at first.

Hagalaz encourages us to look at all challenges that come our way as opportunities for greater learning and growth. The result depends on how you perceive the trials of life. With each step you take, you will grow stronger and stronger to overcome obstacles.

Naudhiz

Pronounced: nowd-heez
Astrological: Taurus/Scorpio/Sagittarius/Capricorn
Tarot: The Devil
Element: Earth/Fire
Key Words: Need, Self-Preservation, Restriction,
                Innovation

Naudhiz is the tenth Rune and the second Rune of the second Aett.

The word 'Naudhiz' represents 'needs' in all their forms, from the roof over our heads, to putting food on the table and also the need for personal fulfilment. If you are not feeling fulfilled in your life, using visualisation techniques is the only way that you can achieve personal fulfilment. We are also encouraged by this Rune that needing and wanting are not the same thing.

Drawing the symbol of Naudhiz next to what you want to achieve will bring you closer to the life goals that you have set yourself.

When we cast Naudhiz, it reminds us that if we push against our Wyrd, which means fate, it may delay us even further in getting where we really want to be. Yet fate deals us a different set of cards to contend with. Our past actions create consequences and we may feel that fate is being cruel and not kind. This Rune represents the obstacles we create for ourselves as well as those we encounter in the world around us. If we shift our perspective and look at our obstacles in a different light, we will find a different understanding in how we can overcome them.

When you cast this Rune, you may be feeling that your life is out of sync and nothing seems to be going right. Life may seem more complicated than it needs to be and somehow we convince ourselves to run around at 100 miles an hour. You may also feel that you are spending the majority of your time on things that do not matter to you. Take a step back and look at what is going on around you; don't ignore your gut feelings, especially if you feel that you are going down the wrong path in life.

The symbol of Naudhiz can also represent that we are at a crossroads in life and not sure which direction to go in. This may be a time when it is more appropriate to slow down and not try to force things that you want to happen. If we force things to happen beyond their natural order and timing, we will find ourselves back at square one, having to learn the lesson again. We must remember at this time that asking for help is not a sign of weakness; it's a sign of strength. This is also a good time to exercise patience.

Our Norse ancestors believed that this Rune cannot be reversed or turned upside down, but can lie in opposition. This means that this Rune enhances and strengthens the others in their meanings.

Isa

Pronounced: ee-sa
Astrological: Sagittarius
Tarot: The Hermit
Element: Water/Fire
Key Words: Life feels Static, Unmoving, Stillness,
                  Temporary Delay

Isa is the eleventh Rune and the third Rune of the second Aett. The traditional meaning of Isa is ice, and the symbol represents the icicle. This Rune is connected with the Frost Giants. In Norse myths they started out as icicles, they were huge, evil and they hated the Gods.

Our ancestors saw Isa representing the present moment in time. They used the power of Isa to slow down surrounding energies to create calmness around them.

This Rune indicates a period of rest before beginning new activities. We may learn meditation as this can also be a time to reflect on all of our achievements. This period of stagnation could also be a time for you to get in touch with your spiritual side.

We may, however, feel that we cannot stand still, but sometimes it is important to put our future plans on hold until a more favourable time; all things will come to us when the timing is right. If we do decide to push against this stagnant period, we will come up against obstacles and life will appear to be out of sync; nothing will feel as if it's going right.

No matter how much you have, you may feel that it is never enough, and when this Rune is cast there is an ever-present desire for something more, something better. Yet whatever we do to get moving again, to bring those things into our lives, Isa will bring things to a halt, and we see our plans suspended. This may leave you feeling powerless in present situations. It could also feel that you have no energy, as you look at the world through dark lenses. This could be because you are disconnected from your own inner power or your chakras are out of balance. There are many ways for you to restore your *'inner power'*, and balance the chakras at the same time. For me, I use *'Journaling'*, as it is one of the easiest and most powerful ways to accelerate your energies. You don't have to be a great writer, perfect speller or creative thinker to keep a personal journal. When you do *'Journaling'*, it helps you by getting your thoughts out of your head and onto paper. Pen or keyboard, it does not matter, but it will help you to gain insights into your current life.

Our Norse ancestors believed that this Rune cannot be reversed because it is a straight line.

If you are feeling that your energy is scattered, then this Rune is very good to help us to ground to the Earth energies. If you take even a few minutes a day to practise, you'll not only have better energy in your daily life, you'll be able to ground quickly. A grounding visualisation can be helpful. Hold the Rune in your hand and use the image of roots growing out from the sole of each foot deep down into the Earth and then drawing up Earth energy.

Jera

Pronounced: yare-a
Astrological: Gemini/Capricorn/Sagittarius
Tarot: The Fool
Element: Air/Earth
Key Words: Completion, Harvest, Peace, Proper
                  Timing

Jera is the twelfth Rune and the fourth Rune of the second Aett. Its symbol signifies the pattern of interlocking wheat grains on the stalk. Another interpretation of the symbol is that it represents the harvest garland. The word 'Jera' means year/season and refers to the recurring nature of the seasons. It also symbolises the agricultural year, as the lives of the ancient Norse people revolved around the seasons of the year.

The Rune Jera represents growth, transition and evolution, which is a natural progression after the Isa Rune. Positive changes come our way and it is a much needed relief as life may have been stagnant for some time. When we cast this Rune, it can also indicate major turning points in our lives that will influence us in the future. We need to let go of the old ways in order for new ones to take place.

It will bring about a time of happiness, peace and prosperity. Jera also influences the fruition of our long-term goals. Jera can bring justice, peace, and harmony into our lives.

Jera's main teaching lesson is that this is a time for reaping rewards from seeds sown, for ideas in the past, and this represents the Universal Law of Harvest. What was sown will be reaped. If you have put in the hard work, you will be rewarded for it. Yet, if we do not sow ideas or have no desired goals to be reached, we will become lacklustre towards life and not have the enthusiasm to do anything.

Jera is a Rune of patience and refers to life rhythms bringing abundance into our lives. This Rune reminds us that we cannot act against the natural order of things like linear time, calendar dates and the clock. Jera teaches us about being in the right place in the right time, which helps us to complete unfinished business ventures.

When we choose this Rune for meditation, it brings about beneficial results when we connect to our Spirit Guides, and Angels.

As a writer, I cast this Rune as it brings out the best in my abilities to meet my deadlines. It motivates me to push beyond my present abilities as a writer. You may wish to draw the symbol of Jera to invoke positive changes in your life, such as spiritual growth.

Our Norse ancestors believed that this Rune cannot be reversed or turned upside down, but can lie in opposition. This means that this Rune enhances and strengthens the others in their meanings.

Eihwaz

Pronounced: ay-wahz
Astrological: Capricorn/Scorpio
Tarot: The Hanged Man
Element: Earth/Air/ Fire /Water
Key Words: Stability, Trustworthiness, Reliability,
Strength, Dependability, Endurance,
Transformation

Eihwaz is the thirteenth Rune and marks the middle of your journey in learning the Runes. It is the turning point of your quest as your old self falls away and a new one is reborn. It is also the fifth Rune of the second Aett.

Eihwaz represents the World Tree, Yggdrasil, which unites Heaven and Earth. With its roots deep within the dark underworld and its branches high up in the sky, it unites mankind with the Gods. The Germanic peoples connected with the yew on the Winter Solstice on December 21st, as they believed it always reflected eternal consciousness.

Eihwaz takes it names from the yew tree, *Taxus baccata*. The Germanic Rune carvers used yew to make their Runes as they believed it was a sacred and a magical protector which held powers. Talismans were also made from the yew and bows were made to defend themselves and their land. The yew tree also symbolised warmth, as it fed their fires.

This Rune is often called the *'Death Rune'* because of the

number 13 associated with it. Its foreboding reputation is said to date from ancient times. One tale of why the number 13 may be considered unlucky is because there were 13 people, Christ and the 12 Apostles, present at the Last Supper. In some countries, it's still considered unlucky to have 13 people at a table. There's even a name for the fear of the number 13, triskaidekaphobia!

The yew tree has a long association with ancient cultures and is seen as a symbol of life. The yew is known as the tree of death, as they would plant it in cemeteries so it could trap the souls of the dead and act as a guardian against evil and negative forces. Our ancestors believed that if a sprig of yew is placed under the pillow it will ensure that you will meet the person of your dreams who will love and protect you from harm.

Eihwaz is known as a Rune of wisdom and can tap into the mysteries of Yggdrasil. If you choose this Rune in a single casting, it signifies a time when deep, powerful transformations, like a spiritual awakening, will occur. It also heightens our connection with the spiritual realms and our Spirit Guides begin to communicate with us in many ways.

This is also a positive Rune, as it denotes new beginnings and fresh starts. It encourages us to embrace change and make the best use of the opportunities it offers. It allows us to get to the heart of the matter of concerns that weigh heavy on our minds.

Our Norse ancestors believed that this Rune cannot be reversed or turned upside down, but can lie in opposition. This means that this Rune enhances and strengthens the others in their meanings.

Pertho

Pronounced:	per-tho
Astrological:	Capricorn/Aquarius
Tarot:	The Wheel of Fortune
Element:	Water
Key Words:	Mystery, Magic, Rebirth, Psychic Abilities, Prophecies

Pertho is the fourteenth Rune. It is the seventh Rune of the second Aett. The name of this Rune has been translated as *'hearth'*, *'fruit tree'* and *'chessmen'*. This Rune is sacred to Frigg, the Goddess of love, fertility, marriage and motherhood. Frigg is wife to Odin and mother of Balder.

The symbol depicted on this Rune is also thought to have two representations; one is the womb and female fertility, the other is described as the cup of Rune casting and it is tipped to reveal the die which symbolises what life can throw at us.

Pertho is known as the Rune of intuition and mystery. *So, what mysteries have been revealed to you or what secrets do you hold?* This Rune asks that we trust our intuition, even though we may find ourselves in conflict between free will and fate.

This Rune is connected to the three Norns and what the Wyrd (fate) deals us. You may feel sometimes that the Wyrd has control of your life. When you cast this Rune, you may also feel defeated by things that are beyond your control. Being flexible during periods of change is the way forward.

Pertho can be used for different kinds of divinations. It brings us awareness and an understanding of synchronicity. Synchronicity is a term invented by the Swiss psychologist, Dr Carl Jung, to describe a *'meaningful coincidence'* between two things or events. We may find ourselves experiencing these events and also gaining an understanding of how the universe works. You may also feel that you want to hold your cards close to your chest; now is not the time for revelations.

This Rune is connected to ancestry, and your ancestors are a huge part of who, what, where and why you are the way you are today. We need to start with our parents and connect to their parents; *do we know where they came from? Do you know your great grandparents? What happened to them, what challenged them, what made them who they are or were? What happened in the family? Where are your roots?* Patterns, energy, events and burdens from the past are carried down and are repeated through generations, leaving an emotional, physical and spiritual imprint on the individual as they follow the fates of those that have gone before.

Pertho is also the Rune of companionship, family and friends. This is a Rune that portrays happier times spent with the family at events that will leave a lasting impression.

Pertho is known as the Rune of meditation and this can help you to stand back and watch what's going on in your life. Meditation will help you see clearly and fully, without being swept away by emotions, and appreciate the reality of the current situation. Meditation is a practice. It is like practising football, or playing tennis. The more time you spend doing it the better you will become.

You may wish to ask your Guardian Angel in meditation to bring peace into the situations that make you feel vulnerable.

Drawing the symbol Pertho on a piece of coloured card will help to enhance your intuition, as it helps you to connect with your Spirit Guides and Angels. The Norse people wore Pertho as a talisman to help with their divination and enhance psychic powers.

Algiz/Elhaz

Pronounced:	el-hahz
Astrological:	Aquarius/Cancer/Pisces
Tarot:	The Moon
Element:	Air
Key Words:	Protection, Warding, Self-Defence

Algiz/Elhaz is the fifteenth Rune of the set and the seventh Rune in the second Aett. Algiz/Elhaz means 'elk', and the shape of the antler horns is illustrated on this Rune. The name 'elk' is connected with the old Norse word 'elgr'. Our ancestors would follow a herd of elk as they were likely to survive the scarce food supply during the harsh winter months.

This Rune also has an alternative name, 'Algiz', which means sanctuary or temple. Many say that there are several interpretations for this Rune, which makes it the most difficult Rune to understand.

The God Heimdall, son of Odin, Guardian of the Gods, is connected to this Rune. He is known as the God of light. He is also the keeper of the Bifröst Bridge, which is a burning rainbow bridge between Midgard (realm of man) and Asgard (the realm of the Gods). Another God connected to this Rune is Freyr, who is Freya's twin brother. He is known as the horned God of fertility. Ragnarok was the doom of the Gods and men and heralded the destruction of the Nine Worlds. Freyr lived in

Alfheim, where he ruled over the Light Elves. It was said that the last battle he fought with an elk horn as his weapon was at Ragnarok. In Norse mythology, Gungir, which means *'swaying one'*, is Odin's magical spear. Odin would carry his spear whilst hunting elk.

Algiz/Elhaz is the Rune that brings us concerns about security, protection and defence. When we cast this Rune, it asks us, *'Is there anyone pushing you into doing something against your will?'*

As this is a Rune of protection, this will come from external forces such as the Angelic realm. You may feel the Angelic realm supporting you in all aspects of your life's journey. The Angels can help you to connect to and feel Angelic guidance on a daily basis.

You may also feel that your creative influences are blocked. It may mean that all you need is to create the space to focus on what your needs/aspirations are.

When you cast this Rune, you may feel the urge to protect the ones that you hold close. You may feel a need to listen to your intuition, follow your gut feeling and feel safe in the knowledge that you are protected and secure. You may also be feeling that you wish to hibernate from the world to gather some *'me time'* to recharge your batteries.

If you find yourself coming under psychic attack, you will need to take steps to look after yourself by using this Rune for protection. A psychic attack is an energy or a thought form that someone sends with the conscious or unconscious intention to inflict harm upon you. It may be directed towards your emotional, physical, spiritual or mental state. Those negative energies can be projected by drawing the symbol Elhaz on a piece of card; this will help to expel negative energies and influences.

Sowulo/Sowilo

Pronounced: so-wee-lo
Astrological: Aquarius/Pisces
Tarot: The Sun
Element   Fire
Key Words: Good Fortune, Energy, Victory

Sowulo/Sowilo is the sixteenth Rune of the set and the eighth, and final, Rune in the second Aett. The word Sowulo/Sowilo comes from the Germanic word meaning '*sun*'. The same name exists in all three Rune Poems. Its symbol is a ray shining down from the sun, a lightning bolt, spark of life.

During the long harsh winters, the sun appears only rarely, shedding its rays over the fields of ice and snow. The sun was very important to the ancients as they spent a good part of the year in twilight and another part in endless dawn.

The Norse Goddess of the sun, '*Sunna*' also known as '*Sól*', is also connected to this Rune. She is the daughter of Mundilfari and Glaur, and wife of Glen. Every day Sunna was given the task of riding through the heavens on her chariot. Her horses, Allsvinn (which means very fast) and Arvak (which means early rising), pulled her chariot carrying and radiating the sun's light on her chariot. She is chased by Skoll, the supernatural wolf that desires to devour her. It is said in Norse mythology that solar eclipses signified that Skoll had almost caught up to her. Skoll caught up with Sunna on the day of Ragnarok to eat her and she was to be replaced by her daughter.

Guido von List used this Rune in his Armanen Runes. He changed the concept of the meaning of the sun to victory.

In World War Two, this is the Rune that was modified by Karl Wiligut, a Nazi occultist who pushed his beliefs in the Third Reich. He used two symbols of what are now called the Sig Runes for the Schutz-Staffel badge.

Sowulo/Sowilo reminds us that the Sun is our source of external light and warmth, which energises every cell in our bodies and illuminates your mind with positive energy, good health, success and power. This Rune reminds us of what successes we have achieved. Health and happiness are also associated with this Rune, as we feel we can resolve our problems with ease. This Rune also can bring out our leadership abilities, which can empower and inspire others to find their life's calling.

This Rune is connected to our spiritual awakening and consciousness, as the sun's energy gives us clear vision. When we embrace the light with strength, but have also acknowledged, experienced and integrated our own shadow/weakness, then we gain consciousness and empowerment in the world.

This Rune has no reverse meaning. The energy of this Rune signifies your own power and strengths as new starts unfold. These new beginnings ultimately bring changes that you can adapt to.

When this Rune is cast in a reading, you will become more aware of your creative potential. This should be developed if you hope to gain your goals in life, as it is the sun that illuminates our thoughts and ideas.

As this Rune is connected to the sun's energy, it can be used for healing. If you are feeling tired and have no energy, drawing Sowulo/Sowilo on a piece of card can give you a zap of energy which allows you to carry on. This symbol can also be used in meditation and to empower the chakras.

The Third Aett – Tyr

Teiwaz

Pronounced:	tee-wahz
Astrological:	Pisces/Libra
Tarot:	Justice
Element:	Air
Key Words:	Justice, Courage, Honour, Duty, Discipline, Strength

Teiwaz is the seventeenth Rune of the set and the first Rune in the third Aett. In Norse mythology, this Rune is connected to Tyr the God of war. He was the son of Odin and Frigg. Tyr fought at Ragnarok, where he battled with Garm, the watchdog of the Underworld. His name gave rise to the name Tiwesdaeg and is given to the third day of the week, Tuesday.

The monstrous wolf, Fenrir, became very powerful and the Gods decided to imprison him. They brought him to Asgard where they could monitor his every move. As no ordinary chain could restrain Fenrir, the Gods created a magical restraint. Tyr, however, dared to feed him and put his right hand in the mouth of the wolf as a sign of goodwill. When Fenrir realised that he had been tricked, and that he could not free himself, he bit off Tyr's hand.

Teiwaz is one of the oldest Runes in the Elder Futhark. It has remained unchanged from early Bronze Age rock carvings. The symbol was often painted on shields to protect warriors when they went into battle. The Norse wore it as an Amulet to protect them from evil forces.

This Rune represents personal sacrifice; you have to keep going until you get through to the result that you want. Teiwaz encourages us that this may be the time to stand and fight for what you believe in and know to be right. When we cast this Rune, it reminds us that we will need much courage in facing and dealing with situations that come our way. Our passions will be our driving force to keep us going. Teiwaz represents our inner strength, our ethics and our honour. It gives us the confidence and dedication to see things through to the end.

Berkana

Pronounced:	ber-kah-na
Astrological:	Pisces/Aries/Virgo
Tarot:	The Empress
Element:	Earth
Key Words:	Mother, Fertility, Goddess, Feminine

Berkana is the eighteenth Rune of the set and the second Rune in the third Aett. The symbol is said to represent the breasts of Mother Earth and of the birch tree.

The word '*Berkana*' comes from the Germanic word for the name for this Rune. It is also known as '*beorc*' in the Anglo-Saxon Rune Poem and '*bjarkan*' in Old Norse. Berkana's traditional meaning is associated with the birch tree. The word '*birch*' is thought to have derived from the Sanskrit word '*bhurga*', meaning a '*tree whose bark is used to write upon*'. The poet S.T. Coleridge called the birch tree the '*Lady of the Woods*'.

Three Norse Gods have an association with the birch tree: Frigg the Goddess of love and fertility, Freya the Goddess of beauty, and Thor the God of thunder and rain and farming. The birch tree is consecrated to Thor because rain was essential to spring growth. The wood was only harvested from the tree if it had been struck by lightning, as they feared it would only anger Thor if they cut them down.

The Norse people would plant a new birch tree before a house was built to protect the home and its occupants. Birch twigs were also used to bestow fertility on cattle and newlyweds. The Rune Berkana represented new life, new growth and new beginnings. It is also known as the Birth Rune and if you are pregnant, drawing this symbol on a piece of card will help you to focus on a positive birth experience.

When we cast Berkana in a reading, it reminds us not to think about the past or let it become an obstacle and hold us back from where we need to be in life. When we let go of what no longer serves us, we will be able to receive and appreciate new opportunities and adventures in life. Many doors of opportunity are opening up for you at this time. There is much energy around and this could prove to be a very exciting time. There is great activity and motion.

Berkana can also indicate that we are entering a period of healing. Whether it is physical, emotional, mental or spiritual, we will come out of the other side feeling stronger and consumed by the need to search for a meaning in our lives.

Berkana can also indicate that this is a time to sow seeds and make plans. You will not see instant results and immediate rewards for your efforts, but do not allow this to discourage you – it is merely indicating that a different concept or angle must be looked at. We are also reminded that our new ideas and concepts need nurturing, feeding and growth before they come into fruition. Patience is needed here and you need to remember that plans, ideas and concepts are not a waste of your time and effort.

Ehwaz

Pronounced: eh-wahz
Astrological: Aries/ Gemini
Tarot: The Lovers
Element: Earth
Key Words: Transformation, Change, Initiation,
                  Confrontation of Fears

Ehwaz is the nineteenth Rune of the set and the third Rune in the third Aett. The word *'Ehwaz'* means horse. It represents two Norse myths that contain horses: Odin's eight-legged horse, Sleipnir, who carried Odin between the Nine Worlds and could gallop through the air and over the sea, and the Goddess Sunna's horses, Allsvinn and Arvak, who pulled her chariot, carrying and radiating the sun's light through the heavens. The symbol is also said to represent two horses facing each other.

In ancient times, the Norse people considered horses as sacred and never took them for granted, as they recognised their importance in many ways, such as in battle, working the land and as the main mode of transportation.

The Ehwaz Rune symbolises our inner strength and can also indicate the spiritual journey that we are currently on. It can represent a transition in our spiritual growth. You may also be awakening your spiritual growth for the very first time. This indicates a very important life transition, as you open up to your spiritual development. The Rune also indicates meeting like-minded people on your journey of spiritual exploration to find out for yourself what is true for you and who you are, as you gain insight into your spiritual growth from a new perspective.

Ehwaz also represents movement in all areas of your life. You may feel that you are closing in on reaching your current goals and life feels that it is changing for the better. Harmony with work colleagues should come easy for you at this time. Ehwaz indicates that we may be thinking of changing our current situation, such as a new job, career or even house move. You may benefit also in the development of an idea for a new business venture or a creative project that you have had an idea for.

When this Rune is cast, you may be feeling that things appear unclear in your life and you feel that you may be losing your way. You may want to re-examine your values and your goals, as it could be that you are lacking the energy to keep on going with current trends that you are faced with. This Rune may indicate that you need to make new connections in order to get tasks finished, as it will help you to overcome all obstacles.

The symbol Ehwaz can be drawn on a piece of card to help you to deal with the changes/difficulties in your life.

Mannaz

Pronounced: man-naz
Astrological: Aries/Taurus
Tarot: The Magician
Element: Air
Key Words: Man, Human, Identity, Self-Realisation

Mannaz is the twentieth Rune of the set and the fourth Rune in the third Aett.

Mannaz comes from the Germanic word '*manwaz*' and the Old Norse word '*maðr*'. All three Rune Poems refer to the relationship between humanity and dust or Earth.

According to Norse myths, the first human beings were made from trees. Askr, the first man, came from an ash tree and Embla, the first woman, came from an elm tree.

Mannaz symbolises basic human qualities and cooperation. It is referred to as a Rune of the mind and of knowing oneself. It also represents supporting others, as well as duty and responsibility. It represents our individuality and you may be feeling that this is the right time not to follow the crowd anymore but to go it alone.

The Rune symbolises the human race/mankind, regardless of age or colour, and represents both male and female. This is a Rune of family and friends, young and old. This may be a time when you fondly recall past times spent with family and friends.

When you cast this Rune, it suggests that you may need to

spend more time thinking about your requirements for happiness instead of another's.

Mannaz also represents our self-knowledge and insight from past lives. You can tap into your past life knowledge through meditation and turn it into positive action. Positive action creates wisdom, and wisdom can untie karmic bonds. This represents a time that you are open to receiving.

This is a Rune that represents our desire for change as we search for the inner self. It also suggests that it is time to balance your mind, body, spirit and soul. *Are you busy with so many tasks that you must do that you have no time for yourself to enjoy your spare time?* If so, you may feel that it is time to make changes in your life, so you have more '*me time*' to do the things you want to do.

This Rune may also indicate that you may have been your own worst enemy. Are you holding on to a firm belief that separates you from success? The Rune reminds you to focus all your energies to make what you do a success, one act at a time.

Mannaz is the Rune of assistance and team work. Good advice will come your way for any new business ideas, and this a really good time to implement any plans.

This Rune may also indicate times when you have been feeling isolated and lonely. At the time this experience strikes, it can be hard to imagine that anything will ever change. You may ask yourself why you are feeling like this. At times, we may become isolated due to circumstances beyond our control. We may also experience loneliness when we have many people around us. Sometimes, the best way to make the first step towards positive alteration of circumstances is to explore what opportunities are available to you.

Laguz

Pronounced: lah-gooz
Astrological: Taurus
Tarot: The Star
Element: Water
Key Words: Psychic Abilities, Flow,
                 Emotions, Spiritual Counselling

Laguz is the twenty-first Rune of the set and the fifth Rune in the third Aett.

Laguz means water, lake. In the Anglo-Saxon Rune Poem it is called *'lagu'*, which means *'Ocean'*. In the Younger Futhark, the Rune is called *'lögr'*, which means *'waterfall'* in Icelandic, and *'water'* in Norse.

This Rune is sacred to Njord, God of the sea, ships and hidden treasures. He lived by the sea at Noatun harbour and was married to Skadi, a mountain Goddess, the Queen of the Snow and Goddess of Hunting.

The word *'Laukaz'* also means *'leek'*, which is derived from the Old Norse name *'Laukr'*. Leeks, *'ítrlaukr'*, were often given to a young man when he had proven himself as a warrior.

Laguz is the water Rune and symbolises all forms of water: rivers, springs, oceans, lakes. Water is associated with emotions of all kinds and this can also be interpreted as the possibility of our losses, our emotions and our fears in life.

Laguz represents the Well of Wyrd. The three Norns drew

water from the well and they poured it over Yggdrasil so that the branches would not rot. This Rune holds all the secrets of the unconscious mind, intuition and mystery. It also represents our psychic, spiritual abilities. Laguz acts like a spiritual counsellor, as it encourages us to look at and understand what it is that is stopping our spiritual development or developing it further. It can be suggestive to have the courage to follow your heart and trust your intuition. Intuition is the most valuable tool you have; follow your intuitive voice, and be guided by your feelings.

Laguz can also represent our emotions bubbling under the surface. Listen to your inner mind, listen to your heart and connect with your emotions.

You may be experiencing a period of confusion in your life, as you feel that you are stuck in a rut and making the wrong decisions. This could be that Laguz also represents emotional cleansing and when this Rune is cast in a reading, it creates opportunities for us to confront our own fears and emotions.

Laguz can also represent spiritual growth. As you may be working with spiritual energies, you may find yourself beginning to dream about the spiritual realm. When you choose this Rune in a single casting, it may indicate that you are establishing a communications link with your Spirit Guides.

This Rune encourages us to go with the flow of life, as Laguz means water. If you go against the ebb and flow of the tide, it may cause resistance, which produces disempowerment. Be guided by your feelings to go in the right direction in life.

This Rune can be used in meditation, as it encourages us to find a deeper understanding of the self and be open to new possibilities. It will attract strength and energy into your life.

Inguz

Pronounced: eeeng-goowz
Astrological: Taurus/Gemini
Tarot: Judgement
Element: Earth/Water
Key Words: Fertility, Resting, Internal Growth,
Harmony, Peace, Unity

Inguz is the twenty-second Rune of the set and the sixth Rune in the third Aett. The word *'Inguz'* means *'fire'*, *'lighthouse'* or *'firewood'*, and survives in the English word *'inglenook'*. To avoid confusion, Rune casters have used two different symbols to represent this Rune. For some, the solid shape of a central tilted square is used. Others use 'X's stacked on top of each other and touching. Both are Inguz.

Inguz represents the Norse Hero-God, Ing, also called Freyr, who brought peace and prosperity, enabling the land to flourish. This Rune symbolises the aspect of male fertility, grounding us to our natural connection with the land. Inguz has a creative and unifying power that has a conclusive result, one that may be linked to projects, ideas and even teams of people reaching their full potential. Matters come to a head and problems are finally resolved.

Inguz is a positive Rune and encourages you to live in the moment. Living in the moment means you are totally immersed in an experience. The energy of this Rune encourages you to think back on the events in your life that you vividly remember. Those are the events where you were living in the moment. Even though years have passed, you can still remember the details. Living in the moment takes practice, because maybe you are used to being distracted and keeping a journal to record the moments when you were totally present.

The Rune can help with grounding ourselves to the earth's energy. The energy helps us to reconnect, rethink and re-link with our spiritual selves. Increasing your natural energies will help you to access your intuition and make informed choices.

Inguz is known as the completion Rune. The appearance of this Rune indicates new beginnings. You may need to remember that when something ends, something new begins. You may find the energy and motivation to start something new, making a clean sweep in all aspects of life so that ideas that you have had for a long time can be turned into a new project. If you are lacking confidence to start something new, then you may like to focus on what you can do and not worry about what you cannot do. Building your self-confidence will maximise your strengths and open you up to learning new things and unleashing hidden abilities.

There are four parts to every person, and Inguz helps you to integrate the four selves (physical, mental, emotional and spiritual) into your everyday life. If you cast this Rune when you may be feeling confused, look at this Rune as a catalyst to know that you are on the right path in life.

The symbol of Inguz can be drawn on a piece of coloured card of your choice to aid our spiritual growth and to encourage good health and restore spiritual balance. It also gives you the energy to find the strength and personal power to complete issues that have been a burden.

Dagaz

Pronounced:	dah-gahz
Astrological:	Gemini/Cancer
Tarot:	Temperance
Element:	Earth /Air
Key Words:	Awakening, Awareness

Dagaz is the twenty-third Rune of the set and the seventh Rune in the third Aett. The word *'Dagaz'* is called *'Daeg'* (day) in the Anglo-Saxon Rune Poem. This Rune is also part of the Elder Futhark. The symbol on the Rune represents the first rays of the sun rising over the horizon. The expression, *'Det dagas'* (which means *'day is breaking'*; the sun is coming back after a long dark night) still exists today in the modern Swedish language. This Rune is connected to the God Heimdall, the God of light.

The Norse people believed that the fresh light of a new day brought them prosperity. As Dagaz means day, this Rune reminds you that you are very close to making a breakthrough to ongoing life dilemmas. You have the determination to change whatever you deem necessary. You also may see the world differently and with clarity at this time.

Dagaz awakens the light within you. As each new day dawns, and the light becomes brighter and stronger, so does the light within you. You may feel a distinct feeling of the lifting and absence of inner burdens, and natural self-healing abilities emerge that were not there before.

The energy of this Rune releases you from self-limiting beliefs, allowing you to access your own truth, unearth your own answers, and awaken to your spiritual path.

Dagaz is the Rune of spiritual awakening. This is a very positive Rune when cast in a single reading. The time is right to embark upon new projects. New possibilities and new opportunities arise as balance has been achieved in your life. It signifies brightness, growth, progress, development and fundamental changes. The power of change is directed by your own free will.

Dagaz reminds us that this is a life of balance – positive and negative, dark and light, night and day. This is the Rune of transformation, the power which is available to all of us. It can also signify the end of gloomy times, and when we step out into the lightness of life, our successes are within reach.

You may wish to draw the symbol of Dagaz to increase your wealth, abundance, prosperity and manifestation. Dagaz can also be drawn to bring a positive outcome to any situation that is of concern to you at this moment in time. This Rune does not have a reversed meaning as it indicates that optimism is the way forward.

Othila/Othala

Pronounced: oh-thee-la, oath-awe-law
Astrological: Capricorn/ Taurus/ Virgo/Gemini
Tarot: The Moon
Element: Earth
Key Words: Communication, Divine Inspiration,
Spiritual Power, Estate, Inheritance,
Household

Othala is the twenty-fourth Rune of the set and the eighth Rune in the third Aett. The word *'Othala'* can be traced back to certain words in Anglo-Saxon and Norse whose oldest meaning is *'noble'* or *'nobility'*, and are associatively linked to *'property'*, *'estate'* and *'homeland'*. In the Anglo-Saxon Rune Poem, the name appears as *'ethel'* (*ēðel*). The God connected to this Rune is Odin.

This Rune is also known as Othila and Odal. The symbol was used to express faith in the Pagan religion of Odinism and was originally a symbol of the Vikings. The symbol below was used as the emblem of the 7th SS Volunteer Mountain Division Prinz

Eugen, operating during World War Two in the National Socialist German-sponsored Independent State of Croatia. The Hitler Youth and the Race and Settlement Main Office also used this symbol.

Its symbol is a house with its roof and doors. The ancient meaning of this Rune is the ancient clans. Today, it is connected with families and your ancestral heritage. You may feel that this is the time to discover where your family came from and unlock the many mysteries about your ancestors; you may be able to prove or disprove family legends.

This Rune may also indicate family disputes and break-ups, problems with parents, children and siblings. It may also highlight possible arguments that are connected to any inheritance.

Othala is the Rune of wealth. By drawing the symbol on a piece of card, it will help you to create unlimited abundance, prosperity and inner peace.

When this Rune is cast in a reading, it is seen as a positive one and can act as an accelerator in our spiritual growth. It can also assist us when we strike a balance between the material and spiritual aspects of our lives.

This Rune may also indicate to us that we want to break the family chains of karma. This Rune encourages the individual to break the endless cycle of frustrations of why things go wrong for family members. It may just be the right time to re-evaluate things. You have to be objective about the situation. Begin by being honest with yourself about your own role in the relationships that you have with your family. You may find yourself in a rut, but making a change in your routine may feel artificial. However, changes will go a long way towards preventing you from becoming and feeling stuck in life.

You may wish to draw the symbol Othala, as this can empower our relationships with family and friends. The energy of the Rune can assist our spiritual and physical journeys.

Chapter Five

The Blank Rune/Wyrd

This life's dim windows of the soul
Distorts the heavens from pole to pole
And leads you to believe a lie
When you see with, not through, the eye
William Blake

Pronounced: No Pronunciation
Astrological: Mercury
Element: Air
Key Words: The Unknown

In 1982, the Blank Rune was created by Ralph Blum, author of *The Book of Runes*. It is suggested that, in the 1970s, the idea of the Blank Rune came from a handmade Rune set he bought in England. He did not use them for a few years, until one day he came across them and started to use them.

In his book, Ralph Blum introduced millions of readers to this ancient form of divination. He recreated the traditional Rune stones and placed them into a different sequence, and suggested that you read the Runes from right to left.

Throughout the years, the use of the Blank Rune in a Rune set is the subject of much highly controversial debate. Some believe it should not ever be used in your Rune casting; others state that the use of this Rune was lost and rediscovered by Ralph Blum. Yet many believe that our ancestors did not use the Blank Rune as there is little or no historical support. For some experts who do Numerology, they believe that having twenty-four runes makes it the correct way, because twenty-four divides neatly into three Aetts. The blank Rune has no set that it fits into. Further opinions have been put forward that there are twenty-four hours in a day, twelve months in a year and eight recognised festivals in modern Pagan and Wiccan tradition, Nordic as well as Celtic.

The Blank Rune, however, has now been used for so long that it is recognised in most books about Runes and sets of Runes available for sale. Today, the Blank Rune is also known as Odin's Rune. The other name of this Rune is *'Wyrd'*, pronounced *'weird'*, which is the collective name given to the Norns. In Norse mythology, the Norns were three Goddesses who ruled over the karma that each person has accrued during their incarnation. They are called Urd, Verdandi and Skuld, and represent the aspects of past, present and future. The Blank Rune is said to have represented Fate, a connection with your destiny, the end of something and the beginning of something new. The answers that we seek to unanswered questions lie within us.

When we cast this Rune, it indicates to us that our own spiritual development is progressing. It also offers a reminder that our own knowledge is greater and stronger than we think.

Our own fears of failure and success rise to the surface, but this Rune encourages us to face our fears, look at them and have the courage to change them. Why not look at this Rune as a blank page for you to start writing down the life you are going to create. Remember only you can do that when you are ready to do so and make of it what you will.

From my own experience, some of my students, who follow tradition and stick to rules, often take out the Blank Rune before a casting takes place. Other students think of the Blank Rune as a *'spare'* in case they lose one.

Personally, I do not use the Blank Rune myself as, like my students, I also prefer traditional methods, but I have included it in this book for those who are interested. I am going to leave it up to each individual reader of this book to use or reject the Blank Rune – trust your intuition.

Chapter Six

Runes That Cannot Be Reversed

Around here, however, we don't look backwards for very long. We keep moving forward, opening new doors, and doing new things, because we're curious and curiosity keeps leading us down new paths.
Walt Disney

From my own experience when you are using the Tarot cards, they can be reversed if you choose to use them in such a way. It is the same way for the Rune stones; some of us cast our Runes, tipping out the whole set and letting them fall as they may. Others pull Runes from the bag, usually one at a time. Either way, the Runes do not always come out upright and face up.

Many books on Rune interpretations see any reversal of a Rune as negative, often describing it as '*Myrkstave*' which means dark and gloomy as opposed to '*bright*' when in the upright position.

However, you need to be aware that some Runes appear the same when you turn them 180 degrees and are always '*upright*' no matter which way they land. The following Runes that will always appear '*upright*' are: *Gebo, Hagalaz, Isa, Jera, Eihwaz, Sowilo, Inguz, Dagaz* and the *Blank Rune* which is also known as the *Wyrd*.

They can, though, lie in opposition, which means that they can lie sideways or off-centre. Some even have the capability to distort rather than enhance the meaning and message of the Runes on either side of it.

When casting the Runes, it is helpful to have a system of deciding which Runes you will consider upright, and which you will consider reversed. I usually interpret all the Runes with their top pointing up or to the left, upright; and all the Runes that have their top pointing down or to the right, reversed.

It is believed that reversed Runes often point to an aspect of ourselves that we may have been unwilling to face, but which we are now ready to acknowledge. When this happens we may often choose totally new directions for ourselves, reaching a point where we can transform and empower ourselves to keep moving forward.

Chapter Seven

Making Your Own Rune Set

The spiritual path is simply the journey of living our lives.
Everyone is on a spiritual path; most people just don't know it.
Marianne Williamson

In ancient times the spoken word was more important than writing. Laws, religion, customs, history, including stories about Gods and other supernatural beings, were handed down from generation to generation by word of mouth.

Writing was limited to the use of Runes and the Vikings used many materials to make their Runes, such as bone, stone, deer antlers, ivory and wood.

You may want to buy your own Rune set from the internet or high street shops. But if you would like a Rune set that is more personal and more powerful then why not make your own.

There are countless benefits from making your own Rune set. The Runes that you make yourself will inspire your connection with this ancient art form and help you to become more accurate and clearer in your readings.

Making your own Runes can be as simple or as complex as you want it to be.

Different items used will have distinct magical qualities. Choose an item that feels right for you at that moment in time. You can use pebbles, stones, sea shells, beads, glass stones, wood or any other material that speaks to you. Using your creativity and intuition, you can collect things from places that have a sacred, mythical meaning that inspires you.

For those who do pottery and ceramics, clay is a fantastic substance for your personal Runes, as you can easily shape the pieces and inscribe the symbols before they go into the kiln for firing.

The points below will help you to create your own Runes.

1. Collect smooth stones from the garden, or pebbles from a beach, garden centre or craft shop. If you do not wish to use those items, you may want to use your own crystals or buy some from shops. Whatever object you choose, they should be flat and smooth on one surface for you to apply the Rune symbol.

2. There are Rune Card sets available to buy. You may want to use this idea and use gold or silver marker pens and write a Rune symbol on each of the cards. You also may want to use different colour cards for the three different Aetts. You could also go one step further and illustrate the cards with drawings having some reference to the meaning of each Rune to help you remember the significance.

3. You may want to make your Runes from salt dough or craft dough. The art of salt dough can be dated as far back as Egyptian times. Salt and wheat flour were the most common foods available to them. The materials needed to make the dough are inexpensive, which you will probably find in your kitchen cupboard.

4. If you cannot find any nice stones to use, you may also use small pieces of wood for your Rune set. To keep them authentic, you may need to cut the Runes into 1.25 cm disks and sand all the surfaces of each one to smooth out the wood. Using a pencil, etch on each symbol against the grain of the wood.

5. If you have decided to use stones for your Runes, wash the stones to remove any residual salt, water, sand and dirt. Dry your chosen items with a towel.

6. Using an acrylic paint colour of your choice (henna also works well), paint your symbol on the smooth surface of each object. Some of my students have used gold or silver

leaf on their Runes and they have found it to be a very effective decoration. What colour paint you use to draw the symbols is entirely up to you – allow your intuition to guide you.

7. Once dry, you may want to spray or paint a clear protective coating on your finished Runes. You could use yacht varnish, which can be bought from department stores. A bottle of clear nail varnish can also be used to bring out the natural colours of each stone.

8. You may want to place the Runes on the window sill in the sun for a day or under a full moon to attune them to your personal vibrations and energies. Regular charging will keep the energy of the Rune stones focused on positive energies.

9. You may want to create a simple drawstring bag of any material to store your Runes in when not in use. This can also be bought from high street shops and the internet. Whatever you decide to do, make sure you have ample room to get your hand in and out of the bag and space to hold your casting cloth.

10. Casting cloth – In ancient times, a piece of white cloth was used to cast the Runes. These can be bought from bookshops or the internet. You may wish to make your own and buy a large piece of material of your choice and cut it into a square. You may want to decorate the outer side of the cloth with Rune symbols and draw, paint or sew a circle in the middle in which to cast your runes.

Many people use Runes as a tool for personal growth and meditation. They are also a useful tool for bringing relaxation into your life. They can help you look at yourself and situations differently. Feel free to experiment, be creative and most of all have fun!

About the Author

Kylie Holmes, a naturally intuitive person, has refined her skills through regular meditation, self-development techniques and MBS-related courses. Mother of four Old Souls, she is also a writer, an Intuitive Angel Therapist, Intuitive Writer, Reiki Master and Past-Life Regression Therapist.

Kylie's website is: www.touchedbyanangel.me.uk

Email: kylie.holmes@btinternet.com

Moon Books

PAGANISM & SHAMANISM

What is Paganism? A religion, a spirituality, an alternative
belief system, nature worship? You can find support for all
these definitions (and many more) in dictionaries,
encyclopaedias, and text books of religion, but subscribe to
any one and the truth will evade you. Above all Paganism is a
creative pursuit, an encounter with reality, an exploration of
meaning and an expression of the soul. Druids, Heathens,
Wiccans and others, all contribute their insights and literary
riches to the Pagan tradition. Moon Books invites you to begin
or to deepen your own encounter, right here, right now.
If you have enjoyed this book, why not tell other readers by
posting a review on your preferred book site.

Recent bestsellers from Moon Books are:

Journey to the Dark Goddess
How to Return to Your Soul
Jane Meredith
Discover the powerful secrets of the Dark Goddess and transform your depression, grief and pain into healing and integration.
Paperback: 978-1-84694-677-6 ebook: 978-1-78099-223-5

Shamanic Reiki
Expanded Ways of Working with Universal Life Force Energy
Llyn Roberts, Robert Levy
Shamanism and Reiki are each powerful ways of healing; together, their power multiplies. *Shamanic Reiki* introduces techniques to help healers and Reiki practitioners tap ancient healing wisdom.
Paperback: 978-1-84694-037-8 ebook: 978-1-84694-650-9

Pagan Portals – The Awen Alone
Walking the Path of the Solitary Druid
Joanna van der Hoeven
An introductory guide for the solitary Druid, *The Awen Alone* will accompany you as you explore, and seek out your own place within the natural world.
Paperback: 978-1-78279-547-6 ebook: 978-1-78279-546-9

A Kitchen Witch's World of Magical Herbs & Plants
Rachel Patterson
A journey into the magical world of herbs and plants, filled with magical uses, folklore, history and practical magic. By popular writer, blogger and kitchen witch, Tansy Firedragon.
Paperback: 978-1-78279-621-3 ebook: 978-1-78279-620-6

Naming the Goddess
Trevor Greenfield
Naming the Goddess is written by over eighty adherents and scholars of Goddess and Goddess Spirituality.
Paperback: 978-1-78279-476-9 ebook: 978-1-78279-475-2

Shapeshifting into Higher Consciousness
Heal and Transform Yourself and Our World with Ancient Shamanic and Modern Methods
Llyn Roberts
Ancient and modern methods that you can use every day to transform yourself and make a positive difference in the world.
Paperback: 978-1-84694-843-5 ebook: 978-1-84694-844-2

Readers of ebooks can buy or view any of these bestsellers by clicking on the live link in the title. Most titles are published in paperback and as an ebook. Paperbacks are available in traditional bookshops. Both print and ebook formats are available online.

Find more titles and sign up to our readers' newsletter at http://www.johnhuntpublishing.com/paganism
Follow us on Facebook at
https://www.facebook.com/MoonBooks
and Twitter at https://twitter.com/MoonBooksJHP